ALSO BY TERRI APTER

The
Confident
Child

RAISING A CHILD TO TRY, LEARN, AND CARE

Terri Apter

W. W. NORTON & COMPANY · NEW YORK · LONDON

Library of Congress Catalog Card Number: 96-36180

ISBN: 0-393-04058-5 (hardcover)

ISBN-13: 978-0-393-32896-7 pbk.
ISBN-10: 0-393-32896-1 pbk.

W. W. Norton & Company, Inc.
500 Fifth Avenue, New York, N.Y. 10110
www.wwnorton.com

W. W. Norton & Company Ltd.
Castle House, 75/76 Wells Street, London W1T 3QT

1 2 3 4 5 6 7 8 9 0

for **Miranda, Julia, Brian, and Adrienne**

Acknowledgments

I wish to thank the parents and children who attended my workshops in Cambridge, shared their problems, and tested solutions with me. Their optimism, humor, warmth, and trust were crucial to shaping this book. In the course of the past ten years, ongoing conversations with my sister, Marion Quinn, persuaded me that parents needed a book to help them motivate and support their children. Together we mused over the difficulty of sustaining a very young child's exuberant confidence through the challenges of middle childhood. As parents, we felt that in our most important job we faced an obstacle course through which we wanted to preserve a child's goodness, while shaping character. We pooled observations about effective methods of discipline. We wondered how we would sustain our influence as our children made their way in school and among peers. Geographical distance did nothing to impede these conversations, but I wanted to give them a broader canvas and a research-based structure.

This aim was facilitated by conversations I had with Judy Dunn and by her work on the connections between emotion and under-standing in development. Her ability to combine theoretical so-phistication with day-to-day observations helped structure my sense of the important ways parents can pass on their knowledge about emotions to children. Jim Gilligan's searching questions about the importance of self-esteem inspired me at a time when I had only the vaguest notion of embarking on this project. Through-out the past ten years, Nancy Chodorow, Mary Jacobus, Michelle Stanworth, Sandra Gilbert, and Mary Hamer have offered essen-tial reality checks to problems and questions that have arisen in our mutual—but very different—parenting experiences. I see this book not as an end, but as a continuation of such conversations that are going on between parents everywhere.

My agent, Meg Ruley, was always available as a sounding board for my ideas, and her attention has been invaluable. My editor, Jill Bialosky, while experiencing one of the most demanding phases of parenthood herself, continued to parent this project with her ex-pert guidance and support.

Contents

The **Confident** Child

one

Confidence for Life

Building Blocks

Many years ago, as a sophomore in college, I worked as an assistant on a study of children's motivation. My job consisted of greeting the child and parent as they arrived at the research unit, handing the parent a permission and information form to fill in, and seating them in the room in which the study was to take place. After two further parent/child couples went through the same process, I brought out a large box filled with wood blocks of different colors, sizes, and shapes, and explained to the children, who ranged from two to five years of age, that they were to build the best tower they could build with these blocks, and that someone would judge which child's tower was really the best. The parents were then led from the room. I told the children when to begin, when to stop, and gave a signal for the "judge"—a Ph.D. student—to enter. He studied the towers closely, nodded from time to time, muttered to himself, and took notes. He then declared one to be "the best" or "the winning tower." This process was repeated three or four times before the session was declared to be at an end.

This procedure in fact had nothing whatsoever to do with assessing children's skills in building towers. The declaration that a tower "won" was random. The aim of the study was to observe children's responses to success or failure. Their responses were filmed, and then analyzed by the researchers in charge. I did not see the films, but these scenes have never ceased their re-runs inside my mind.

When I began this job, I knew nothing about, and had no feeling for how children liked to be treated, for what adult behavior might be convincing or threatening or disturbing, for how children might be responding to the world around them. But the P.R. part I played was deemed inadequate by my employers for other reasons: I "disturbed" the study by comforting the losing child; I was insufficiently "neutral" as I described the process of the "game"; I sent messages to the children, even before they began, that the game should not be taken seriously.

It was not the youngest children who roused my empathy. The two- and three-year-olds were in some ways hard work, because they often had their own ideas about what they wanted to do with the blocks, or whether they wanted to play with them at all, but on the whole, their "winning" or "losing" was of little import to them. Most of these very young children seemed to note their success or failure dispassionately. "Oh," they might say, with a shudder of surprise, either to winning or losing; and whether they won or lost, they took great pleasure in demolishing the structure with one swipe. Some who won expressed surprise, and looked at their towers with new respect. A few did, even at age three, seem disappointed or angry. But the crestfallen face or the stamp of rage was transient. Within minutes, they were back into the "game." Disappointment simply did not stick to them.

It was the slightly older children whose behavior turned my routine into torture. When these children "lost," a cloud descended upon them. One girl sat with her eyes fixed on her tower and touched it gently with the tip of her forefinger, up and down, as though to protect it. When I spoke to her, she seemed too embarrassed to face me. A boy who had constructed his tower with the utmost concentration, knelt beside his "losing" structure and gazed at it from beneath, humming to himself as he dismantled it, slowly, brick by brick. He then stirred the wooden blocks into a pile as though to remove any sign of his former efforts. After two or three such "failures to win," the children became sullen and withdrawn and discouraged. They did not want to build another tower, they lost hope of winning and were irritated by my attempts to encourage them.

The oldest children in the study—the five-year-olds—were enormously pleased when they won, but they also showed increasing despair at losing. After being told that his tower "won," a child raised his eyes from his own work and looked triumphantly at the loser. His body stretched, his hands were thrown high, his pride swelled. The losing child, on the other hand, seemed to shrink. He crouched down, focusing mournfully on his "losing" tower. Another child tried to cover her mood with an embarrassed smile. Her mouth was fixed into a stiff grin, and her eyes filled with tears. Some children were better at controlling their feelings, but the pain was still evident. One child looked at the winner with a forced smile, but hunched low and hugged her ankles. Another's attempt at a smile was foiled by the twitching of her mouth, and the quick pulling in of her lower lip. When I coaxed her into reluctant speech, her voice was dull. Hearing her voice crack, she ceased speaking.

At the time, all those years ago, I think I was ashamed not so much of my participation in that cruel study but, strangely, of my knowledge as to how cruel it was, and how closely I identified with the children who lost. Surely, the successful college student would not share this knowledge of constant and confused failure. Surely, if I had been the sort of person I then wanted to be, I would not have been so close to their experiences of being crushed by competition. Their unguarded expressions of pain brought home the unrelenting tension of my daily life and the question that nags every adolescent: If there are so many people who are smarter, more talented, more clearly focused than I, why should I keep trying and caring? I saw in them what I longed to be rid of: that sense of my deepest self being crowded out by my own inadequacies and others' excellence. For these children now being socialized into the world I was experiencing, all I could do was signal that the judge's verdict did not matter. I could, at least, stave off the day they might discover that it did.

What I must have known then, but ignored, was the fact that such competitive situations are inevitable. The young children who participated in that study were experiencing no more or less than they would in the classroom or on the playground. What I must have known, but then ignored, was that their suffering was a pale precursor to the struggles that older children engage in, as they build up their knowledge of skill, effort, and ability. Much later, as a parent, I colluded with this competitive world. Like many parents, I taught my children that doing well was important and that failures had to be overcome. Like many parents, in my children's own best interests, I taught them to worry about their performance in school and on national exams. I insisted that to develop the skills they needed to thrive, they must sometimes win, and therefore I taught them to think better of themselves when they won than when they lost. However firmly convinced I was that they were of value no matter what, and that I would love them no matter what, I could feel anger, despair, or depression if they did not seem to be on track toward gaining the skills that are judged to be necessary to a good life. The college student who felt outraged that any child should be subjected to such a cruel competition became the typical parent caught between the need to help her children develop their potential, and the wish that they be happy just being themselves.

This daily battle to attain a balance between teaching children that they must do their best, and teaching them that they are "the best" regardless of what they do, is an inevitable tension in parenting. We do have to teach our children how to achieve, and we do have to encourage them to feel better about achieving than failing. We do have to work on their behalf—and sometimes against their inclinations—to inspire them to develop their potential. But while we do this, we risk making them feel awful about themselves. This self-defeat can consume enormous energy as a child seeks to protect herself from its blows. The child can create disguises and defenses that blind us to her real feelings and real needs. To help our children sustain that vital confidence that motivates them and fills them with hope for their future selves, we have to understand what self-esteem is. For self-esteem is the key to a child's bright future. But what is it, and how is it maintained?

Self-esteem is now recognized as a key to children's successful development. It is crucial to who children are and who they aim to become. Self-esteem has a far greater impact than intelligence or innate ability. Children who believe that they are valuable and effective, and who have the skills to behave in accord with these beliefs, have higher expectations of future successes, persist longer in tasks, and show higher levels of overall performance than other children, equally able, but less confident. *Emotional intelligence,* which is a crucial part of self-esteem, gives a child resilience and enables her to tolerate frustration, so that she can engage in sustained effort. This special form of intelligence also involves awareness of how her behavior affects other people, thereby inspiring concern for others and responsibility for her actions. These skills ground children as people who can live positively with others and achieve personal satisfaction in an increasingly complex and demanding society.

In our current and future cultures, people will need even greater inner strength to withstand change and uncertainty. We have to help our children find ways of valuing themselves and caring for others even when they face disappointments. Few of today's children, it is expected, will have life-time jobs. Employment will never be as secure as it was a generation ago. Skills demanded in any business or profession are proliferating and changing: Adults, in tomorrow's society, will need to be flexible and adaptable and capable of meeting constantly changing challenges. They will require greater confidence and flexibility than we did, however competitive and crowded we may be finding our own adult world. Our children, as adults, will have to develop new ways of working together and conserving the environment. They will need to stand firm against increasing violence and social division. We need to pass on to our children a variety of ways of feeling proud so they do not have to resort to destructive ways of feeling proud. It is dangerous to suppose that they will simply "toughen up" or learn how to "handle difficulty." We can depend on this: If a child does not have self-esteem—which means valuing her future and believing that she can influence her future—then there are two outcomes: depression or destruction. Depression stems from a sense of helplessness, from repeated experiences of failure and lack of control, and destructiveness is a violent defense against this helplessness as one vents anger against one's loss of control and potential.

Self-esteem is not a single idea or feeling or belief. It is not constant self-admiration or even self-love, but rather the presumption that one should persevere, take responsibility, make a positive difference to one's environment. **Self esteem is a set of skills that allows a child to keep trying, to keep learning, and to keep caring.** These are skills that allow us to keep bouncing back when we experience disappointment, frustration, or failure, and to sustain positive engagement with other people. Too many programs meant to encourage self-esteem plug positive thinking and a barrage of self-praise: a child is instructed to tell herself she is "terrific" and "lovable." Such purely ego-boosting practices leave the reality a child experiences—and needs to experience—out of account. As William Damon, an expert on the moral development of children, writes:

> Children are remarkably bright and active when it comes to figuring out who they are. They have a searching understanding of self that few adults fully appreciate. They are aware of what they can and can't do; and they constantly probe their surroundings for feedback about their capabilities.

No self-esteem guide should ignore the reality of a child's self discoveries. Nor, as we try to help our children sustain good faith in themselves, should we minimize the important role that their disappointments and frustrations take in their development of personal strength and stamina. When we talk about a child's self-esteem we are dealing with high stakes: our own child's future and the future of our society. As parents and people who care about a human future, we cannot afford *not* to understand how to sustain our children's self-esteem.

Many books on self-esteem are addressed to adults who feel the need to develop, or reinforce, or recapture their own self-esteem. Adults who have lost their self-esteem somewhere along the road to maturity are assured they can repair past losses and take greater control of their lives by repossessing the self-confidence and self-appreciation that was damaged at an earlier phase of development. Such books try to treat those childhood wounds that, once inflicted, leave scars that fester throughout adulthood. They help us trace our way back to earlier turning points, amending the wrong steps taken. Yet surprisingly little has been written about what we as parents can do to sustain the self-esteem of our children (especially that of children past the infant and toddler stage), to allow our children to grow to be adults who do not have to do this repair work, since harm was never done. In fact, we understand far more about how self-esteem can be damaged in childhood—through neglect or abuse—than we do about how it can be fostered, preserved, and reinforced.

This book deals with just that. It focuses on the crucial years from five to fifteen, when children learn to assess their abilities and form expectations of success or failure, and when their emotional intelligence is being formed. It addresses parents who want to gain a fuller understanding of how children develop their sense of who they are and how they relate to other people. It suggests ways that parents can spot problems in a child's *self theory* (ideas about who she is, what she is worth, and who she can become) and help the child sustain positive attitudes and correct destructive ones. It also deals with our inevitable imperfections as parents, and suggests ways that we can cushion the effects on our children of our own faults or failings. Since children need control and discipline, as well as freedom, responsibility and praise, I address the problems we, as parents, face in building up children's behavior without breaking down their belief in their basic goodness.

Since children also develop in school, and among siblings and friends, chapters are devoted to the role these experiences and relationships play in the development of self-esteem. In Chapter 6, I describe children's intense fear of failure, and suggest how we can help them through the challenges of classroom humiliations. Sometimes competition and discouragement arise within the family, especially within the context of sibling rivalry. The various responses children commonly have to siblings are described in Chapter 7, as well as suggestions for softening the impact of this frequently brutal struggle for parents' love and approval. Children's friendships play a large role in their sense of self, their sensitivity to others, and their ability to interact positively with people around them. They compare themselves to their friends, and they learn about their own potential for relating to others in the course of passionate childhood friendships. I have therefore included a chapter describing development through friendship. Though we often are not at hand to help a child through the rough and tumble of life with peers, we can provide a child with skills to preserve the friendships she values, and avoid the pressure of those that constrain her. Since the transition from childhood into adolescence is so complex, and so commonly misunderstood, I describe the new difficulties parents face with teenagers, and the ways in which we can work with our teenagers to overcome common misunderstandings. If we keep the lines of communication open, we can continue to help an adolescent build the sense of self that will well serve the adult the child is becoming. Finally, because a person's moral principles play a large part in self-esteem, I show how the skills outlined in this book can be used to meet the challenge to raise a moral child.

I generally refer to the child as "she," but my interest is in boys and girls alike, and—unless I make specific distinctions between boys and girls—the discussion is meant to refer to any child.

The material for this book is drawn from a variety of sources. The work of Erik Erikson remains of enormous value to any description of a developmental "task" or stepping stone along a path of personal growth. The work done by Gerald Patterson and his colleagues at the Oregon Social Learning Center has fascinated me for many years in its careful tracking of parent/child conflict, and I am grateful to them for supplying me with data. The work of Myrna Shure and George Spivack has inspired me with its emphasis on parent/child conversation as a means of drawing out a child's ability to solve her own problems. Daniel Goleman's formulation of emotional intelligence highlighted the ways in which skills and emotions are linked. His work convinced me that this age span—from five to fifteen—is particularly important to address, since it is during these years that a child's emotional intelligence takes shape. Lyn Mikel Brown and Carol Gilligan have revealed how adults' silencing of a child's thoughts, feelings, and desires can have soul-destroying effects. Their work has brought home to me the importance of allowing a child to have her say without being punished or judged or ridiculed.

The examples and practices described in this book come primarily from children and the parents who are struggling to realize their child's potential. From 1990 to 1995 I ran a series of workshops in which children of various ages were observed at home, in the classroom, and on the playground. Parents sometimes came to me with problems they had spotted or issues they were concerned about; but sometimes a child's behavior concerned me, and I would then invite the child to speak more fully about her experiences. I always worked with both the child and at least one parent. Whenever a specific problem was discussed and advice given, I tracked the effect on both parent and child. In this way, certain expectations about what could help and what could hinder a child's development of confidence and the potential that is expanded through confidence, were often revised. The quirks of children's minds have a compelling logic. Discovering the forgotten realities of children's experience is a special pleasure, as well as a useful tool for parents. The child's vast hope and anticipation alongside the sense of being "small" and uncertain in a big, challenging world provide a window onto children's minds. It was clear that, for them, self-esteem is not a solid set of beliefs or a fixed psychological foundation, but a continuous process, both delicate and resilient.

Raising children often seems like walking on a minefield. The most cautious step can trigger an awful explosion, whereas an apparently foolish jump can be made without causing damage. Alternatively, we can look at child-rearing as a task in which there are lots of chances and frequent warning signals from which to learn. No book can map a perfectly safe path through that minefield. Each child is different, and each interchange between parent and child is characterized by a deeply personal context. No so-called expert can, in book form, take the rich variety of family life fully into account. I address the reader *parent to parent:* Though I draw on the experience and research of many writers and psychologists, I suggest that each parent makes use of all advice through her knowledge and experience of her own child. By offering descriptions of parenting styles that have often proved effective, I hope to help parents make the best of the many opportunities they usually have. A child's self-esteem is broad and deep and, like a strong, loving relationship, is not always felt in its entirety, but is always reparable. The good will that so many parents have toward their children needs to be harnessed so that cycles of unhappiness—and waste—can be broken.

two

Assessing a Child's Self-Esteem

C hildren's self-esteem normally is not simply high or low. Instead, it is like a layered cloud that undergoes daily shifts in shape and intensity, varying with a child's own mood, the familiarity of the setting, the task at hand, the attitudes of the people around her.

What Self-Esteem Means to Children

The psychologist who has conducted the largest study of children's self-esteem, Stanley Coopersmith, suggested that we imagine self-esteem as a kind of interior monologue a person holds—the self telling a story about the self. In particular, it is about the ability to do things, one's value as a person, and the significance of one's life. When a child does something, does she believe she will do it well? Will she succeed in what she tries to do? How does she measure up to other people? Does she worry about other people knowing more, being smarter or more skilled than she is? Does she worry whether they will like her or find her interesting? Does she wonder, anxiously, whether she will be able to join them in conversation or games or school tasks?

We can, as a rough guide, imagine a child with high self-esteem speaking to herself in the following way:

> I'm a valuable and important person. I am at least as able and good as other people. People who know what I am worth will treat me well. I can make decisions about what to do and what to be, and those decisions count, both because I can carry them through and because what I decide and what I feel influences other people. My thoughts and my feelings matter; they make a difference. The world is full of people to meet and things to do, and I am happy to meet the challenges these different things offer. If I don't succeed in one task, or if one relationship doesn't work out, then others will because I am generally capable of making good friends and doing good work, and I'll keep succeeding in the future.

Life for this child is interesting rather than threatening. But a child with low self-esteem, or who holds what is sometimes called a "negative self-attitude" would think and respond quite differently:

> I am not important, or likeable. I can't do what other people can do, and if someone asks me to do something I won't be able to do it at all, or not in the way anyone thinks I should. I'm the sort of person other people will tease, or ignore, or abuse, and what I want doesn't matter, so I barely know what I want. I hate change, however uncomfortable things are now, because change will confuse me and make demands on me that I cannot meet. I don't have any control over what happens to me in the future; things may get worse but they won't get better.

These two very different monologues map out different attitudes; but in real life children's attitudes are not purely distilled as either one or the other. Until the age of about fifteen, when the self-concept acquires much of its (more or less) permanent structure, children tread a fine line between these two opposing "monologues," stepping from one to the other with disconcerting ease. Their daily lives are chock-a-block with discoveries about their abilities, their powers, and their limitations. They feel confident in one situation, and not in another. It is not simply that, like adults, they know they can do one thing and not another—such as draw a picture of a tree, but not climb one. Their doubts are far more profound and elemental. They are in control of their lives when the school bell rings, but experience a revolution of confidence when someone is late to pick them up. Their world changes every day as does an adult's only in times of social upheaval and war. The ground on which a child stands shifts several times each day.

Not only does children's awareness of what they can do fluctuate, but so too does their sense of how others see them. One minute their behavior arouses delight in those around them; the next moment it invites intense displeasure. Jack, age seven, was happily at play with his younger brother, rubbing a balloon on his sweater, and then watching it stick, unheld, on the two-year-old's hair. His little brother grabbed the balloon, bit it, and burst it. His mother rushed in, and watched the toddler barely able to scream because the balloon skin was stretched across his face. "What the hell are you doing? Don't you know—never, never—to let him put a balloon into his mouth?" "I didn't know! I didn't know!" Jack cried. "Well, you should have known," his mother retorted. "And now you do." "But I didn't know," Jack wailed, his happy world suddenly shattered. He was no longer the good big brother, but the careless enemy.

Even at the age of eleven, Charlie was taken aback by the way a conversation with her mother could break down, and she could switch from being "a good sort of person to something real bad, really in the wrong." "I'm just talking about stuff—like, at breakfast I was making out a birthday list. And Mom's nodding, 'Okay. Make a list.' Then suddenly I get this, *I don't want to hear another word!* Because all of a sudden what I'm doing is some terrible crime, talking about my birthday when she's thinking about getting ready for work and I should be getting ready for school. Okay. I see what's happening. But I don't see it coming."

Children learn that they are agents, acting in the world and influencing things around them; but they also learn that their actions have unexpected consequences. They often learn the hard way, as adults deem them "naughty" or "bad" because their behavior has consequences that they could not know it would have. Sometimes they judge things just right, but often they do not, and they have to negotiate through a morass of injustice and self-pity. They live in the thick of acceptance and rejection—both from the voices of adults who switch from encouragement to anger with bewildering ease, and from friends who promise companionship but rapidly turn into accusers.

Just as uneven in children's daily lives are their experiences of successes and failures. They manage to ace a spelling test, but get a detention for forgetting their science homework. They are praised for their cooperation with a sibling, but are snubbed when they ask a classmate whether they can join a game. And because children seldom distinguish between the big and the small, the larger successes cannot compensate for the minute failures.

If a child's self-esteem normally is so changeable, how can parents tell whether it is strong or weak? How can we know whether our parenting, as it is, is just fine for our child, or whether we need to change some of our parenting strategies in order to preserve our child's confidence? How do we know when our child is coping with these inevitable ups and downs in life, or whether her self-esteem is suffering?

Knowing Our Own Child

By the time a child is five or six, parents think they know her pretty well. We know the patterns of her responses: to a hard day at school, to a good meal, to a lost or broken toy, to a day at the zoo. We know the rhythm of her rise to excitement and her sink into the doldrums. We know when she will be shy and when she will eagerly move forward. But this kind of knowledge may leave us with many gaps in our understanding of how a child is making sense of her world and assessing her position in it. A child of this age can now control many of her feelings. Some of her feelings about herself are so complex that she has no choice other than to contain them—or to express them in oblique ways.

Self-esteem involves a complex set of feelings and beliefs and expectations based on a child's changing skills in interacting with and influencing her world. There is no simple and sure method of assessing a child's self-esteem, or measuring the extent to which a child lacks it. If a child is asked directly whether she thinks she is capable of doing something, or whether she likes herself, she may speak with a confidence that she does not really feel, or she may be expressing a false confidence, one that does not buoy her up in real-life situations. It may sound right to say, "Yes, I'm good at making friends," or she may have learned that she is supposed to say good things about herself. In the abstract, a child may believe the positive things she says; but when actually confronted with a friend-making situation, self-doubt may be activated and suppress this ability she believes she has. Elaine, nine, described herself as "very good" at math, but was tongue-tied when the teacher called on her in class, and she explained a failure in a math test as a result of "my mind freezing even though the answers are there." She may well be right, but if she is not helped to find ways of identifying what she cannot do and dealing with her deficits, the "answers" trapped beneath the frozen mind will soon disappear. A child may believe that she can do great things—win medals as a gymnast, become President, fly the space shuttle—but not feel sufficiently confident to join a playground game or a school chess club. When eight-year-old Joe was asked about his tennis skills, he declared himself to be "the next Arthur Ashe," yet he refused to participate in a school tournament. A dream is not supportive if a child is afraid to test it by taking steps to realize it. Children's positive self-attitudes are of little use unless they have everyday access to them.

Because self-esteem is so complex, and so tricky to assess, I offer in this chapter a long check list of possible signs of low self-esteem. This check list offers parents some idea of the range of behavior and attitudes that might be cause for concern. This list was compiled by Peter Gurney through his extensive work with children both as a teacher and a psychologist, and is suitable for children between the ages of five and fifteen. Since children are different in the home, with friends, and at school, there are three headings. Remember, this list is intended to *guide* a parent's assessment, it is not a scare list. All children will sometimes exhibit some of the characteristics on this list. Highs and lows in self-esteem are, after all, part of a normal child's experience. Parents should use this list to assess the different areas in which a child needs help.

At home, the child with low self-esteem may behave in any of the following ways:

- *wishes she were someone else*

    A longing to be someone else may show itself with excessive day-dreaming, or wishing to be younger and therefore relieved of the demands of maturity. The most marked and disturbing sign of this desire to be someone else is lying about things that would make a difference to who she is: For example, she tells her friends or teachers elaborate stories about how she lives or what has happened to her.

- *feels inferior or unworthy*

    This can be seen in a child's low expectations of others' responses to her. She may seldom seek others' attention. She may become distressed when someone shows an interest in her. Admiration may confuse her—even to the point of tears.

- *cries frequently when faced with new or difficult tasks*

    Some children have an intolerance of difficult tasks and constant anxiety about how they will perform. This can lead to frequent bouts of tears.

- *makes negative or derogatory comments about herself*

    Most parents are accustomed to hearing their children make exaggerated claims for their abilities. A child with low self-esteem, however, may claim to "hate herself" or "wish she were dead."

- *lacks energy*

    Most children seem to burst with energy, but a child who feels helpless sees no point to trying. Moreover, a child who feels constantly anxious may be drained of energy. Sometimes such children even move slowly because they feel helpless or uncertain.

• *cannot tolerate ambiguity*

When a child lacks confidence in her own judgment, she will want everything to be spelled out—over and over again: She does not believe she will be able to understand anything that is not completely plain or simple. She may also be anxious about the consequences of misunderstanding. For example, if you ask a child to help the babysitter put her brother to bed, or take a phone message, or return a library book, she may be so worried she will not do something "right" that she is afraid to accept the responsibility of doing anything. "What if my brother cries?" or "What if I can't understand what the person's saying?" or "I don't know how!" she may protest, even though she is clearly capable of doing these things. A child with strong self-esteem, however, will be aware of her abilities, and less worried that something will confuse her.

• *is self-destructive/self-mutilating*

Some children who claim to hate themselves may actually inflict harm upon themselves—usually by biting or scratching. A "clumsy" or "accident-prone" child may harm herself without thinking. Sometimes a child harms herself to get attention, which she feels she cannot get by any other, more positive route.

• *is poorly dressed and groomed*

This is common enough in children who have all too many other things to think about. But poor grooming *can* be a sign that a child does not enjoy thinking about herself or does not care about herself.

• *finds it difficult to make decisions*

This is another sign that a child lacks faith in her judgment and is anxious about the outcome of any choice. For such a child, choice, which should be empowering, only serves to remind her of what she is afraid she cannot do.

• *takes a pessimistic view of her future*

It is disturbing to hear a young person speak with dullness or despondency about her future. Yet some children see "nothing much" ahead, and therefore "don't care what happens."

Among other children, a child with low self-esteem will exhibit some of these behaviors:

• *bullies smaller/weaker children*

A child who feels weak herself, and is frustrated by lack of confidence, may try to feel powerful by frightening other children, especially those who frighten easily. She may want a companion in her fear, or she may want to appear "tough" to disguise her sense of powerlessness.

• *acts aggressively toward peers*

Some very good childhood friends are routinely aggressive to one another, but systematic aggression to a wide range of other children is a sign of a disturbing, general dislike of one's peers. It was Aristotle who first suggested that liking for others depends on a liking for oneself. A child who wants to push other children away may be afraid that others will push her away.

• *lacks confidence with strange adults or new peers*

Shyness is common in children and is often linked to the temperament with which they are born. But if a child freezes up with any but the most familiar people, she may be afraid that new people will see her as "bad" or "inept." Such intense shyness— or an inability to express oneself and link up to new people—is also a concern because it can *lead* to low self-esteem. A child's sense of her social competence, or incompetence, plays an important role in establishing confidence.

- *finds difficulty in seeing others' points of view*

On the whole, children are quick to "read" people's thoughts and feelings; but this ability can be dulled by a child's belief that she cannot understand other people, or that there is little point in trying to monitor their views. If she has low self-esteem, she may give up trying to understand people.

- *is over-dependent on opinions of authority figures or high status peers*

A child who does not trust her own judgment, or is unable to act on her own initiative, tends to follow others who seem confident. A child who has no inner direction will choose friends who order her around, and will find authoritative adults attractive. Such a child craves other highly confident people, and relies on their instructions or ideas instead of developing her own.

- *gives away little personal information*

A child with low self-esteem assumes that she is of little interest to other people, and hence will not bother to reveal anything about herself. She will assume her ideas and feelings do not matter and that no one wants to hear of them. Again, this can be a *sign* of low self-esteem, but it can also *lead* to low self-esteem. When a child is slow to express her thoughts or feelings, she cannot influence others' decisions about where to go or what games to play. She therefore will have little experience of positive impact among peers.

- *avoids leadership roles*

A child with low self-esteem will often believe that she is incapable of organizing others or participating in decisions.

- *rarely volunteers*

A child who feels that she has little to offer, or is unlikely to act competently or satisfactorily, will not offer to participate in anything. She may also assume that people do not want her help, that they have already judged her and found her wanting.

- *is often withdrawn/socially isolated*

   Believing that she does not know how to get other children's attention or keep them entertained, a child with low self-esteem may withdraw from other children. If she does try to join a group, her efforts are likely to be awkward and ineffective.

- *is rarely chosen by other peers*

   One of the most disturbing things about low self-esteem in children is that it becomes a system of interlocking beliefs and attitudes which then is self-maintaining. A child who rarely volunteers, who offers little information about her thoughts and feelings, who does not reveal her ideas but depends upon directives from others, will rarely be chosen for games or teams or pair work. She is not particularly fun to be with, and seldom contributes to group spirit. Her experience then confirms her lack of confidence.

- *behaves inconsistently*

   When a child does not trust her own judgment, or when she lacks appropriate self-control, she may behave inconsistently. She may, for example, be very quiet on the playground, when she believes she will not successfully engage other children's attention, and boisterous in the classroom, when she knows that her behavior will attract the teacher's attention. Or, she may misread certain situations. Teasing children may seem friendly to her, and a friendly gesture may confuse her, so she responds inappropriately. For example, she may follow a tease around, hoping to make friends, but be unresponsive to a friendly gesture, thereby giving up the possibility of making a real friend.

- *appears submissive/lacks assertiveness*

   When a child is unaware that she is of value, she will submit to others' whims and orders. She may believe that it is natural for her to do what others tell her to do, and that her only chance of finding a place among her peers is in a submissive role.

- *attracts attention to herself*

    Low self-esteem has many different and apparently contra-dictory manifestations. Some children, who think they are worth little and have little to offer, draw attention to themselves by boasting—about birthday parties, pets, parents' attainments, new purchases. Some children constantly clown or disrupt other children's games because they see no positive way of getting attention.

- *rarely laughs or smiles*

    A child with low self-esteem often feels anxious—worried that she will let someone down, that she will not understand what is demanded of her, that others will for some reason or other dislike her. The "frozen" face of some children with low self-esteem stems from this anxiety.

- *makes derogatory remarks about peers*

    When a child feels that she will not gain approval, she may take comfort in condemning others. She may complain about another child who is "rude and dirty," "a bitch," "real stupid," or "a fool." She finds comfort in looking down at others: If only, she believes, other people will join her in condemning someone else, they will not condemn her.

A child may exhibit low self-esteem at school with any of the following behaviors:

- *acts impulsively*

    This is another version of inconsistent behavior. A child who does not trust her judgment, and who is so anxious that she fails to take her time to monitor a situation, often acts before thinking. She may in some way see that her behavior is inappropriate, but she does not see how to improve it.

- *is easily distracted/has a short attention span*

    This characteristic stems from a child's inability to believe that she can complete a challenging task. As soon as the going gets rough—if, for example, she does not immediately understand a reading passage, or cannot quickly solve a mathematical problem—her attention wanders. Frustration is necessary to learning. A confident child can tolerate frustration because she believes it will eventually ease—as she understands what she reads, as she begins to take steps to solve the math problem. A child who lacks confidence experiences frustration as failure.

• *suffers acute anxiety in new situations*

Some children with low self-esteem function well enough in very familiar settings. They may feel that no one will demand too much of them, and that they have worked out ways, in a familiar setting, to deal with the limitations they believe they have. But when a situation changes, they become terribly anxious because they feel different kinds of things will be expected of them. For example, a child may worry that she will not understand the homework instructions of a new teacher, or will not know when it is acceptable to ask to use the toilet.

• *suffers from personal mistakes and goes out of her way to avoid them*

No one likes to make mistakes, but a child with low self-esteem will find them particularly painful because they confirm her sense of inadequacy. A confident child will see a mistake—such as dropping a piece of chalk or making a mistake in the conjugation of a French verb or using a word incorrectly—as a minor mishap, or a fluke, whereas a child with low self-esteem will see the mistakes she makes as confirmation of her ineptness, as typical rather than accidental. In going out of her way to avoid mistakes, however, a child avoids challenges through which she can grow. This is another example of the ways in which low self-esteem becomes part of a self-reinforcing system.

- *lacks motivation*

When a child believes she will not succeed, she sees no point in trying. Motivation rests on the assumption that one can achieve something, or reach a goal; but a child with low levels of confidence feels ultimately helpless.

- *lacks persistence generally*

This characteristic is closely related to a short attention span. Persistence involves continued effort, even when things get difficult. To persist, one has to believe that one has a fair chance of seeing a job through. Low self-esteem, however, involves the belief that one is more likely to fail.

- *follows rigid thinking patterns*

A child with low self-esteem does not expect others to respond sensitively or sympathetically to her, nor does she trust herself to "read" others' expectations or responses. Therefore, she clings to a few set patterns of thought, such as "I must be nice and I must be quiet"—even if the teacher is trying to encourage the children to act out a play. As the math book is opened, she thinks, "This isn't the sort of thing I can do." She sticks with these thoughts simply because they are familiar to her. She rejects new ideas or suggestions—for example, about how to solve a problem or how to tell a story—because she is too anxious to try out new things.

- *seriously underestimates* or *overestimates her abilities*

It may seem strange that a child with low self-esteem may overestimate her abilities, but this is a common defense. She cannot confront her true abilities, and so she creates a fantasy. Also, to compensate for her sense of inadequacy, she may try to believe she is really extremely good at something that is not currently being challenged. She may, for example, believe that she is really an excellent musician or actor or singer, because no one judges her in these areas, whereas she knows she is underachieving academically, because that work is monitored. On the whole, however, a child with low self-esteem is likely to have low expectations of herself because she underestimates her abilities.

• *sees success as the result of something outside her self*

This characteristic is terribly frustrating to people who are trying to help a child raise her self-esteem. When a child with low self-esteem does well on an exam, or wins a race, she will say she did well because "it was easy" or because "the teacher liked her" or because she was "lucky." A confident child will say that she did well because she was "smart" or "knew the stuff" or "worked hard." The confident child who does well sees her good work as a source of pride, and a confirmation of her abilities, but the child with low self-esteem cannot even use a successful experience—such as doing well on a test or scoring a goal—as a resource of self-confidence, because she does not take credit for it.

• *sees failure as a result of something within her self*

But what happens when a child fails? A confident child will see failure as a one-off event. She will say that she did not do well because she had a headache, or the exam was too hard, or the teacher was unfair—or because, this time, she did not study enough. But a child with low self-esteem will see failure as the direct result of her lack of intelligence or talent. She will explain that she "isn't good at that," or that she is "stupid." Her unhappy experiences will enforce her sense of inadequacy, but her experiences of a positive outcome will not boost her confidence because she sees the reasons for good performance as stemming from things outside her—luck, the teacher's feelings, a "too easy" exam.

• *assumes negative experience is typical*

As if this persistence in seeing herself as inept were not bad enough, the child with low self-esteem thinks that one failure is a sign of future failures. "I always get these problems wrong," or "I always do stupid things like that," are common responses in children with low self-esteem.

• *finds it difficult to work independently*

   The child with low self-esteem may become dependent on bossy peers and authoritative adults because she wants others to tell her what to do. For the same reason—lack of faith in her own initiative—she would prefer not to work on her own in school. She often asks others what she should do, or whether what she is doing is "okay" because she is unsure she understands the assignment, or is slow to believe she can do it satisfactorily.

• *asks few questions*

   At the same time she craves others' help with her work, she may, in some situations, ask too few questions. She may refrain from asking them because she is afraid of appearing stupid, or she may simply be unsure that she can get someone's attention, make herself understood, and understand the reply. For the same reason, she rarely answers teachers' questions. Even when she knows the answer, she is unsure whether her answer is the one that is expected.

This check list does not offer a straightforward scale for measuring the severity of a child's problem in the way a thermometer measures the extent of a fever. If one child exhibits nine characteristics on this list, and another child exhibits only three, this does not mean that the self-esteem of the first child is three times lower than that of the second child. The severity and persistence of each symptom should also be taken into account. A child who sometimes feels "down" and discouraged may be very different from a child who has low self-expectations even when she seems relatively content. The point of this list is not to ring alarm bells, but to help parents observe a child's behavior and reflect on its possible range of meanings. If a group of characteristics on this list is displayed by a child, then a parent can use the following discussions in this book to draw a provisional map of the child's problems, gain understanding of them, and—most important of all—intervene in a positive way.

three

Helping a Child Overcome Low Self-Esteem

The First Target: Anxiety

P arents can save a child from low self-esteem and prevent a child's natural "downs" and doubts from turning into low self-esteem, but positive action has to be well-considered and systematic. Low self-esteem is self-reinforcing, which means if a child has it, she will probably keep it. We cannot target one symptom on its own, because these symptoms are interlocked. A child who believes she is not good at math will be flooded with anxiety when faced with a difficult math problem; unable to work at the problem, she will experience another failure, and thus enforce her belief that she has no mathematical ability. A child who believes that she is unlikeable will be reluctant to approach others; she will then lack experiences through which she can develop interpersonal skills. She will remain unable to interact positively with others, and will continue to experience rejection. But before I go on to describe the ways in which we can teach a child specific skills to improve behavior, effort, and outlook, I want to focus on the **emotions** that lock children into patterns of low self-esteem.

These emotional impediments to self-esteem will be targeted from many different angles throughout this book: For if we are to teach our child how to set goals and work toward them, we must alleviate the feelings that glue negative thoughts together. When we work with a child to develop her *emotional intelligence*—that is, the positive use of emotions to control her behavior, communicate her feelings, and respond effectively to the feelings of others—we can change the problematic beliefs and expectations that accompany and reinforce poor self-esteem. To help our child develop emotional intelligence we can engage in what psychologist John Gottman calls *emotional coaching*. This involves:

- talking to children about their feelings and those of others
- showing acceptance of those feelings
- helping them find acceptable ways of expressing their feelings

To begin this important task, we need to understand how emotions both hinder and help self-esteem.

HOW ANXIETY ARISES FROM LOW SELF-ESTEEM

A child is anxious because she thinks she will fail and be punished or suffer humiliation for that failure. A child who is anxious about failing, does not want to try out new things, and feels comfortable only in the most familiar and well-tried situations. To stave off self-doubt, she may crave a rigid schedule and have rituals to create some semblance of control and order because she lacks confidence in her abilities. Every time she makes a mistake—or sees herself, perhaps unjustifiably, as making a mistake—she blames herself. As a result, her belief in her general inadequacy is confirmed. Feeling inadequate, she may feel that there is little point to trying. Hence, she lacks motivation. And because she is unmotivated, she will not get the positive feedback she would need to satisfy and stimulate her. Her anxiety, *caused* by low self-esteem, also *reinforces* low self-esteem.

> Martin, age nine, had always had some trouble with math, but was able to get by with hard work. However, when he was introduced to long division in third grade, his teacher expressed concern that he was not able to keep up with the rest of the class. His parents, confident in his ability, worked with him at home. While they cooked or watched television or paid bills, he would sit at a table and do his homework. Sometimes he would ask, "How many times does 9 go into 60?" His mother would try to get him to give her the answer, but after a while her temper would rise. "Think! If you can't remember a number near 60 that is something times 9, then what number clearly does go into 60 that's near 9?" Martin blushed. Tears stung his eyes. "I don't understand a word you're saying." "Then listen!" his father instructed. "I'm listening, but I don't understand. I'm just stupid. I can't do this!"

Martin's anxiety creates a mental block. Terrified of coming up with an incorrect answer, concentration becomes impossible. His father tries to break down this resistance, but his intensity and anger only increase Martin's fear. The boy finally insists that he cannot do the work because he is too anxious to try.

Here are some guidelines for Martin's parents, which could help any anxious child:

- Martin's homework should be done in a quiet room. Noise of any kind can be immensely distracting, and distraction increases anxiety: it adds to the fear that makes concentration difficult.

- When a parent helps Martin, she could sit quietly beside him and keep her voice low. Martin would not then have to cope with the further fear of angering a parent if he made a mistake.
- One way of teaching anxious children to unlearn their paralyzing fears involves re-conceiving mistakes. These mistakes—in school work, in social situations, in games—can be shown to be sources of information. Instead of being condemned, they can be useful feedback. "Let's look at this closely. Good! This shows us what the problem is. Now we can begin to solve it." This can be an effective technique both in the classroom and at home. Instead of labelling something as "wrong," use the mistake as a starting point for solving a new problem: *Learning how to solve problems is essential to the recovery of self-esteem, and making mistakes is an important part of learning how to solve problems.*

A child may also experience anxiety, and a lowering of self-esteem, when she believes she cannot maintain self-control. Such control is crucial to learning and the development of skills. Self-control involves the ability to sit back and think, to make decisions, to reflect upon the possible outcome of our behavior. But an anxious child cannot control her impulses, and therefore cannot develop self-esteem.

Hazel, age eight, cried easily and frequently—over a friend's rejection, or a sister's teasing, or a teacher's strict word. The crying itself became a torment to her, and she dreaded situations in which she might cry. Wiping away her tears, she would demand, "Why am I such a cry baby?" and this query gave rise to further tears.

Her lack of control reinforces her sense that she is not what she wants to be and cannot become what she wants to be. Unable to have adequate control over her behavior, her self dissatisfaction turns into envy—which is the ultimate wish to escape from being herself. Others around her all seem better equipped to express themselves, to control themselves, to think for themselves: if only she could be someone else! Or, maybe, she thinks, things would be better if she were younger, perhaps a baby again, when such uncontrolled behavior would be tolerated, when she had been loved for the very things she hates about herself now. She can imagine overcoming her anxiety only by becoming even weaker than she already is. Yet what she really wants is to be able to trust herself not to be inappropriately and uncontrollably emotional.

Some guidelines for Hazel's parents are:

- Sometimes Hazel should be allowed to "bottom out"—to have her time of tears and tantrum. Then, when she grows quiet and less tense, help her understand what she is doing as she regains her composure. "You're now more calm, and able to be in control. See—you're no longer crying." In this way, *we teach her to learn from herself.*
- Listen to her when she abuses herself with terms such as a "cry baby." A parent of such a child might try saying, "I understand how you hate crying. It seems that you want to be more in control. That's a very grown-up thing to want." A parent can *show her that her dissatisfaction has a positive side.*
- Focus on what she can do and has done. Comparisons can be threatening to a child with delicate self-esteem. Suggest that she think about why she is crying or stomping or screaming, rather than why other children are not.

A child is anxious because she believes that she will not be able to understand what is expected of her. She follows the lead of others and allows them to determine her activities because, in her view, they know more, have better judgment, and should have more say. At school, too, she lacks confidence. She may panic when confronted with a new lesson or a new topic because she does not expect that she will be able to learn. Whereas other children exult in adventure, she avoids risks because she does not expect that she can rise to a challenge. Fearful of risks, she is rigid in her ways and rejects introduction of new material or new approaches. She finds it difficult to work independently because she does not trust her own judgment.

Such anxious children may feel as though they do not fully understand what is expected of them and where they go wrong.

Marissa, age ten, is frozen by other children's strangely acquired knowledge of how to treat their peers. "When someone comes up to me, all I can think is: 'What do I do now?' Other kids just talk—like they get into a *conversation.* I just panic."

Hilda, age eleven, is oppressed by her inability to measure her father's expectations. "Sometimes what I do is just right—you know, perfect-couldn't-be-better sort of thing. Then I'll do what I think is the same, but it turns out to be wrong or bad or real disappointing. So it's like I don't know what I've done until he says something. I can't say what it is myself, you see."

Kevin, age twelve, said that there seems to be "lots of layers of gauze between [him] and what goes on in the classroom." Other children, he thinks, have direct access to instructions and information offered by the teacher and other children, while he feels that "more than half of what's said" is incomprehensible.

Some guidelines for Marissa's, Hilda's, and Kevin's parents are:

- Take time to explain as precisely as possible why one type of behavior is acceptable and another is not. Always focus on the particular behavior, not the child in general. Hilda needs her father to explain why she has done one task well, but another one unsatisfactorily. After all, *she should learn from her mistakes, not be made anxious by them.*

- Sometimes lack of a specific skill arouses anxiety—as does Marissa's inability to enter into a conversation with another child. Skills her parents could help her with in this area are described in Chapter 8; but whenever a child is frozen by such a limitation, we should work with her to *identify the missing skill.* With this approach, the child feels that she can learn something to remove her panic, instead of feeling that there is something essentially wrong with her.

- When a child has trouble processing formal instructions, work with her to *identify the problem.* If her anxiety prevents her from remembering what she has been told to do, then encourage her to use memory-enhancing devices (such as writing things down or using a dictaphone). If she freezes at "big words," encourage her to ask questions. If she panics when a direction or assignment is open-ended, show her how at least two different ways of doing it can be right.

- When a mistake is made, take as much time as possible to go through it and correct it. *Rushing creates its own anxiety.*

- Try offering instructions in a variety of ways. Perhaps verbal instructions confuse a child. Try demonstrating the activity, however simple (even taking a phone message), or show the child what to do by doing it yourself. Some children are much better at understanding by seeing than by hearing. *A child will be more at ease if she knows what is expected of her.*

Some children are anxious because they set very high standards for themselves. They feel they "fail" when they cannot meet their unrealistic expectations. Their intelligence is equal to those more relaxed children who assess themselves highly, but they may seem less bright because their anxiety creates a mental muddle.

Judy, age nine, suffers from uncertainty that does not stem from stupidity, but it makes her feel as though she were stupid. She processes a list of questions with every thing she hears. She needs to know precisely what is meant, if she is to understand anything. The middle of three children, she is aware that her eleven-year-old brother and eight-year-old sister know things she does not, that they get the meaning of jokes and puns that have to be laboriously explained to her, that they can follow instructions that overwhelm and confuse her. When her teacher asked the class to list three important dates between 1400 and 1800, Judy could not do this. The instructions are too general: What kind of important dates? How do other children know what an "important" date is, she wonders? She asks her mother's help with the assignment, and then cries because she is not sure her mother knows what the teacher means. And how is it that her mother and even her older brother, who knows the date of the Pilgrim's landing on Plymouth Rock, understand the question and have access to knowledge that she does not? When her mother asks her to answer the phone, she worries that the person on the other end will use "big words" that she cannot understand. When she is instructed to convey a message—to her father or a babysitter—she has to write it down, frightened that she will forget one word, and that the entire message will cease to make sense. While even her younger sister is keen to pay for the newspaper all by herself in a store, Judy worries that something in the transaction will go wrong, and she will not be able to understand what is expected of her.

Tessa, age ten, draws a detailed picture of a daffodil. She makes a beautiful sketch, and then begins to color it. "How am I going to get the leaves right?" she asks her father. "Mix the paints on a plate," he advises, and then watches her. "Not too dark. Try mixing it with a lighter color. Is it too wet? Dry the brush first," he advises as she puts the wet brush to the paper. The paint then bleeds a little beyond the outline of the leaf. "That's fine. Don't worry," her dad urges, but it is too late. Tessa utters a cry, slams the table, hits her head, and crumples the paper. "I can't do this. I always mess things up." The whining, the despair, and the destruction of her own work send a shaft of irritation through her father who shouts, "Don't you ever say that!"

Tessa has rigid expectations of what she should be doing. She is drawing a splendid picture, but because it is not precisely what she wants, she feels she is failing: She claims she cannot do anything because she is not doing, now, precisely what she intends. Her need for perfection may be self-defeating. Her father tries to persuade her that her effort and work are valuable, but Tessa cannot accept this view. In a perverse attempt to prove to her dad that she has not done anything of value, she destroys what she has done.

Anxiety destroys a child's sense that she herself can control her own actions and responses. A child with low self-esteem believes that she will not be able to perform adequately. She expects that she will disappoint others and herself. This background noise of doubt gives rise to an inability to tolerate ambiguity or imprecision. She is unable to act unless she sees precisely what she is supposed to do: New situations require spontaneity and judgment, but she is too anxious to be spontaneous, and she does not trust her own judgment. She worries about being flooded with regret, or being somehow punished. *Children need help exercising their judgment, making decisions and accepting both the negative and positive consequences.*

Judy's and Tessa's parents could follow these guidelines to help ease their child's anxiety:

- They could offer constant reinforcement or praise—not heavy-handed over-praise ("That's just beautiful!" "Isn't that fantastic!"), which children are quick to criticize, but a minimal assent to what they are doing. This could be in the form of "Yes," "Good," or "Fine" or even just "Mmm-hmm." Such rewarding responses can be effective in easing anxiety, while suggestions may be heard, by an anxious child, as criticism. Remember, the purpose of your comments is to sustain her willingness to keep trying—not to distract her.

- However, since some children experience any parental comments (even positive ones) as an intrusion, a child's responses to comments should be observed: Is she distracted even by your positive comments? Does her distress increase, whatever you say? If so, the child should be left to work on her own as much as possible.

- A child who has difficulty regulating her frustration may need a parent to set time limits on an individual task. Children like Tessa need to be protected from overload, and from the stress of fatigue and hunger, so that though she keeps hold of her high standards, she loses her hope of meeting them. Without this protection, the high standards that should increase self-esteem can actually lower it.

- A parent could ask a child to *clarify her goals*. "What result would you be happy with?" Tessa's parent could ask. Does she want her painting to be as perfect as that done by an eighteenth-century master? Or is she after simple precision?

- Once the goal is clarified, the parent can help a child decide whether such a goal is realistic, and then encourage her to work toward it. Sometimes children who set unrealistically high standards are actually aiming toward multiple goals—and diffuse aims will increase anxiety. *Focusing on one goal at a time reduces anxiety.*

- The parent of an anxious child has to make a special effort to learn self-control, too. It does not help to shout when a child expresses negative feelings. It is not easy for a parent to hear a child say "I'm so stupid!" or "I can't do anything!" but when we then command a child never to speak like that again, we are only reinforcing her anxiety. She feels doubly "bad": She feels bad about herself and she feels bad that her despair has made her parent angry. We have to accept children's negative feelings, even as we work to change them. When Martin and Tessa speak negatively about themselves, their parents could say something like, "You're disappointed in what you've done, but you'll have another chance." In this way, *we can register their feelings of disappointment without sharing these feelings or rejecting the child.*

WHY PARENTS OFTEN FAIL TO RELIEVE A CHILD'S ANXIETY

When we help our child with any task, interactions between parent and child are highly complex. First, we want to believe that our child can perform well. The natural pride and faith a parent has in a child is a spur to encouragement. "I know you are capable of anything," is one strand of a parent's response.

When, however, a child shows that she does have special difficulty in mastering a problem, then parents can easily feel offended. We invest some of our own identity in the child, and may feel personally responsible when the child does not perform to a certain standard. I believe this kind of identity investment—this assumption that how well a child does reflects on us—is inevitable. It is part of love, part of the intimate connection between parent and child, but it also explains why the desire to encourage a child can so easily turn to anger. We may feel: "How dare you, who are part of me, reveal yourself to be stupid?" We may in fact feel terror when we see a child's despair: "How dare you give up on yourself when I value you so highly?" may be the unspoken accusation.

A child's self-despair is often rejected by the parent as wrong, unreasonable, or downright bad. "Why do you keep saying that?" Beth's father demanded of her as she repeated that she would not have a good time on a school outing because she would not be able to do the orienteering work demanded of her. "Stop being so damn negative!" In one sense the parent is clearly right: A child who insists that she cannot do something or, indeed, can never do anything, is engaging in defeatism. She is reinforcing her low self-esteem and establishing a principle whereby effort is useless: If she is bound to fail, then why bother to try? The parent who protests against this behavior *means* to protect a child from despondency; but by refusing to listen to what the child is saying and shouting at her for expressing her feelings, the parent may be reinforcing low self-esteem. By dismissing what a child says, we increase a child's anxiety. She is made to feel that her low self-esteem is shameful. Hence, a downward spiral may be set in motion: In expressing her anxiety she meets with rejection, which confirms her sense that she is inadequate. Instead of being "bullied" out of her negative feelings, she needs an environment in which negative feelings about herself can be expressed, but shown to be unrealistic.

Our aim in dealing with an anxious child is to replace anxiety with a sense of control and confidence. Because we have so much emotional investment in a child's abilities and performance, it is essential to find ways of keeping ourselves calm, too. We should establish a non-threatening environment in which a child can unlearn her fear of mistakes or failures. Instead, she could learn that "mistakes" are not going to harm her or the relationships upon which she depends.

The previous guidelines have been directed at certain types of anxious children. Following are three basic ways parents of any child can ease anxiety:

1. Keep a child's attention focused on the task at hand, and away from the concern about assessing her ability, or about disappointing or displeasing others. Say "You're putting a lot of time into this," rather than "You're so slow." Say "I see you need to work hard to get this right," rather than, "You're not very good at this." Say "What do you hope it will be (sound like/look like/do) when you're finished?" rather than "That's not what it's supposed to be" or even "What's that supposed to be?" A child needs to experience trying, without being judged.

2. The warmth and acceptance that parents feel for a child—mingled, doubtless, with an urge to push her to meet her best potential self—can be emphasized.

   Admire her effort and her industry and focus on the skills she has achieved. Show pleasure in listening to what she has to say. Seek her opinion on a variety of things (whether the tablecloth is straight, whether her little brother is secured in the carseat, or whether the papers are nice and flat in your briefcase). Allow her to make as many of her own decisions as possible—about what color socks to wear, what kind of juice to drink, which piece of homework to do first. Your appreciation of these signs of her individuality and initiative will encourage her to feel valued, not merely "assessed." All children—but an anxious child in particular—needs to be assured that we are interested in how she sees things and that we enjoy her thoughts and imagination.

3. Punishment and threat of punishment, or displays of impatience or irritation, heighten anxiety and should be contained. When a child senses our frustration, she freezes with fear—and sometimes shame. We need to create an environment in which it is safe for her both to try and fail.

All this is easier said than done: Anxious children often arouse a certain type of fury in parents who try to help them. When we understand why a child's anxiety about herself can trigger rage in us, we will be better equipped to handle both our anger and our child's anxiety. Anxiety is an impediment to trust. Parents are often surprised by how their relationship with a child becomes extended once anxiety is eased. These extended, more relaxed relationships can themselves improve self-esteem.

The Second Target: Anger

Another emotion that binds negative attitudes and behavior into low self-esteem is anger. The picture we have drawn of the child with low self-esteem has, thus far, been one of an uncertain, retiring child—difficult, perhaps, because she is negative and moody and whiny, who irritates because she does not respond, and who lacks the eagerness we expect of our children—but nonetheless a child generally wanting to please us. Anger is another very different dimension of low self-esteem. An angry child may seem not to care about pleasing us. She may appear particularly un-anxious about performing well in school or meeting our expectations. She may appear self-confident, and tell us she does not need our help, approval, or support. But angry children badly need our help.

Children have an urge to do well and think well of themselves, and they will feel anger when this need is not met. Anger is aroused:

- when something impedes their performance and achievement
- when they are labeled as "bad," "useless," "spoiled," or "a waste" by those whose opinions they value
- when they feel powerless or out of control

Anger is often a defense against low self-esteem. A child feels anger instead of confronting her own disappointment in herself or admitting her lack of power. Such anger can appear in a number of guises:

- Thinking that she cannot be the good and useful person she would like to be, a child may try to deflect low self-esteem by making others feel bad about themselves. She may bully weaker or smaller children. She may act aggressively toward peers: if she cannot gain from peers support and companionship, she turns them into victims, trying to feel strong in contrast.
- Many angry children feel powerless. Perhaps something very disturbing is going on around them (such as a divorce or problems with family finances). Disturbed by what is happening and unable to control their environment, they try not to feel anything. "Acting tough" is a way of suppressing unpleasant feelings.
- When a child feels that others whom she cares for think ill of her, she may cover her pain with anger. In defense against a parent's disapproval, she may think "I don't care what they think of me." She may even think, "I don't care if I am bad/spoiled/stupid/inconsiderate/lazy."
- Very often, under the rule that children should show respect, or say only what is nice (for example, "If you don't have anything

good to say, then don't say anything"), a child is not allowed to voice a wide range of thoughts and feelings. Thus, her thoughts and feelings seem "wrong" and she is angry at being silenced.

- Since anger can lead to defiant or disruptive behavior, a child may be punished for being angry; hence, her anger (at others' disapproval) increases.

HOW CAN WE HELP AN ANGRY CHILD?

In many ways, the children whose low self-esteem is expressed through anger are the most difficult to help. They push us away and deny their need of us. When we try to talk to them, they may sulk and appear to set their hearts hard against us. When ten-year-old Natalie's mother saw her teasing or bullying other children, she would remind her daughter that she should be tolerant of younger and weaker children; yet what Natalie wanted to attack was their strength—their ability to read and write as she could not.

When Patrick's mother saw how cold and indifferent her eleven-year-old son was to teachers and peers, she tried to teach him the value of consideration; but Patrick was acting cold because his own feelings of compassion were too strong for him to handle.

Debbie's mother was distressed by her eight-year-old's "standoffishness," and accused Debbie of not caring that she routinely disappointed her parents; but Debbie assumed a "don't care" attitude because she found her parents' disapproval so painful.

Helping a child whose low self-esteem is defended or disguised by anger is a painstaking process. With an anxious child, we can try many different tacks at the same time; with an angry child, we must start at the more basic level of finding new lines of communication. The following five steps can get us started on this path:

1. *The first thing we have to do is acknowledge our child's anger without condoning angry behavior.* We are often tempted to respond to anger with anger. When our child hits or bullies another, we are likely to insist that the behavior stop—right now. Our child's display of anger makes us angry. This parental anger is a legitimate way of showing disapproval for her behavior, but we set a poor example if we act out our anger as violently as the child acts out hers. Instead, we can acknowledge our child's feelings, while prohibiting her behavior. We can say, "I see you feel strongly about this, but there has to be a different way of showing it" or "I understand that you're very angry, and that's okay, but that behavior has to stop."

2. *We have to assure the child we want to understand her.* Natalie's mother needs to understand why her daughter hits other children, apparently without provocation. She could state her concern, in a potentially sympathetic voice. For example, she could say, "You hit other children, and you know that's not acceptable. Can we talk about this?" This focuses the child's behavior as a problem the parent wants to understand, rather than as a target of punishment or disapproval.

   Many of us, in our busy and stressful lives, may need to make a special effort to give attention and reassurance to a child who feels that her thoughts or feelings are unacceptable. Natalie may not be able to explain why she hits other children. Patrick may not be able to explain his "coldness." But if children are genuinely encouraged to talk about their feelings, the problems disguised by anger will eventually emerge. If they are slow to talk, you can encourage them to act out their feelings, or draw how they feel. However, if they feel they have a listening and tolerant audience, children are usually able to say what they feel.

3. *We should try to address the problem behind the anger.* Natalie's difficulty in keeping up with the academic standards of her class

does not excuse her behavior: understanding poor behavior is different from condoning it. But as we show her that we know there is a problem behind the behavior, we show faith in her basic goodness and remind her that problems can be explored and solved. By saying "There must be something wrong for you to behave like this," we give the message that she is not naturally, or inevitably bad. We also show her our willingness to help her with the problematic feelings or experiences that give rise to her behavior.

If we show our genuine desire to help, and seek her cooperation, she may well be able to suggest a solution to her problem herself. "I want more help at school," she may say. Or, "I want to do something I can be really good at." Children continually amaze both parents and psychologists with their ability to see solutions to their problems.

4. *We should assure the child that her anger, or whatever lies behind it, will not harm her relationship with us.* Many children are reluctant to bring their thoughts and feelings to our attention because they believe that if they are honest and open, we will be shocked or angry. Children often do not think and feel as we expect them to, or as we think they should, but it is always inappropriate for us to punish them for their thoughts or feelings. We may have to acquire new skills in listening and accepting what they say. This means that when our child says, "I hate going to Grandma's" or "I think Auntie Ruth is ugly," we do not say, "No you don't" or "You don't really mean that" or "How dare you say such a thing." Even if they express views that strike us as biased or cruel, we can hear them, and then explain why we don't share them—but this is different from denying a child's right to voice her thoughts. We can teach her empathy and fairness in a number of ways, as I shall show throughout this book: But we do not teach her empathy and fairness by silencing her.

5. *We have to "listen" to a child's anger—even when that anger is directed toward us.* Sometimes a child is angry at not having enough attention from a parent. Sometimes a parent's routine does not suit the child. It is easy, then, to defend yourself first, by denying that there is just cause for anger, rather than listen to the case against you. It is easy to protest, "I spend lots of time with you!" or "I give you every bit as much attention as your brother!" or "Lots of children have to leave the house at this time in the morning! Why must you always complain?" It may be far more effective, however, to ask the child to help you explore the cause of her anger. By the age of five, a child has enormous capacity to say what she thinks and feels—if only she is allowed to, in a safe environment. This means she needs to know that she will not arouse your anger by explaining how she feels, will not be taunted or mocked or accused (of being "spoiled" or "selfish") when she speaks her mind.

It is often surprising just how inventive a child can be when a parent asks her how things could improve for her. Alice, seven, said, "I just need time alone with you before going to bed," and that may mean about half an hour without the competition of a sibling or a telephone. Craig, six, said, "I need to get up earlier, so I don't have to rush to leave on time." A child who is angry at a parent often wants what is possible and reasonable for that parent to give, and she always wants the parent to understand her.

If we are able to handle a child's anger in these ways, then her anger will be more manageable—both for her and for us. Furthermore, as a parent offers understanding, a child extends her emotional vocabulary: She learns how thoughts are connected to feelings, and she learns that feelings can be managed through understanding. When her anger no longer frightens a parent, she herself may become better at controlling it.

A by-product of these parental efforts may also be that a child's anger is assuaged through the vital attention we give her as we try to develop new routes to understanding and interacting with her. In showing her that her thoughts and feelings and perspective are valued (even though we may not share or agree with them), we offer her a sense of her own significance. A child whose feelings are acknowledged, can learn to use those feelings to make her life better, rather than worse. Emotions then can become a source of empowerment rather than despair.

The Third Target: Depression

The quintessential experience of low self-esteem comes in the form of depression. There is something particularly upsetting about a depressed child. For depression interferes with learning, with play, and with the development of relationships—sometimes even relationships with parents. At a time when life should seem full of promise and when fantasy should be given free rein, however, some children feel they have reached a dead end. The prevalence of depression in adults—especially women—has had much attention in the past few decades, but its prevalence in children has often gone unnoticed. Recent estimates indicate that even in the past three years the number of children suffering from mental illness has doubled. As many as 3%, or 80,000 children in the U.S., and 20,000 in Britain, are suffering from serious clinical depression. Between 5% and 39% of junior high and high school students experience moderate to severe depression. And nothing will pin a child more firmly to poor self-esteem than depression.

Depression is different from unhappiness. It is different from sadness triggered by the death of a pet, or a fight with a friend, or a poor exam result. It is different, too, from those deeper and more generalized bouts of unhappiness that children endure—over a parent's divorce, over changed economic circumstances, over an unsatisfactory school. On a day-to-day basis children can face problems that make them less than happy, but they deal with these as part of the rough and tumble of life. Some children, however, have moods that cannot be so simply defined. They feel "down" or "blue" or simply sad. But these usually pass. We can help them pass. We can cheer a child up by taking her to a movie, or preparing her favorite meal, or just talking with her. Even if her unhappiness lasts a while, her normal life keeps ticking over until the mood passes.

The depressed child, however, does not simply feel down or blue or sad. She suffers profound disruption in how she sees herself and the world around her. She can barely envision herself as happy. She may feel that something is so deeply wrong with her that she does not deserve to be happy. She may think a lot about dying, because, unable to believe she can solve her problems, she simply wants to escape her misery. She may not talk about these thoughts, because she knows they are "bad." She may seem pliant, but be filled with despair. As parents, we need to be aware of the symptoms of depression in children—which are often very different from the symptoms of depression in adults.

THE SIGNS OF DEPRESSION IN A CHILD

Depression is basically a sense of helplessness and hopelessness: A depressed child views herself, her situation, and her future negatively. This mind-set can be expressed in a number of very different ways:

1. *Depressed children may act impulsively.* They do not believe they can solve their problems, so they make little effort to attain self-

control or do sustained work. "I can't make a good, sensible choice about what to do or how to do it, so I'll just do *something* and get it over with," is often the thought behind a depressed child's impulsiveness.

2. *Depressed children believe most of their attempts will end in failure.* They see themselves as the sort of people who are likely to fail at whatever they do, in every sphere of life. At school, they believe they will not understand a teacher's explanations. On the playground, they believe they will not be welcomed in a group game. At home, they feel they burden or bore others. They see failure as a result of who they are, rather than what they do. "I'm not the sort of person who is good at school or who is quick to make friends," a depressed child assumes, whereas a non-depressed child will experience a failure as something that simply happens from time to time, something she can learn to correct. If a non-depressed child is not successful in making one friend, she will try another. Often depressed children refuse to put forth effort, and it may seem to other people that they really do not want to think well of themselves.

3. *Depressed children give away little personal information:* They usually feel they are not worth knowing. Some depressed children become distressed and confused when people try to talk with them: They are certain they will disappoint whoever appears to be interested in them. Or, their reticence may stem from a suspicion of others, a fear that others will disapprove of them. Quick to feel guilt themselves, depressed children are often anxious about other people condemning them for some (often nameless) flaw.

4. *Depressed children do not volunteer because they do not believe their contributions are valuable.* Some depressed children become anxious when they are asked to volunteer—for a school play or project—because they feel a heightened awareness of

their "inadequacy." Other children, when depressed, simply feel invisible, and cannot believe anyone is interested in their participation.

5. *A depressed child expects that she will disappoint people, and hence is withdrawn.* Even if she can make initial contact, she will not follow it through, because she does not expect to sustain someone's affection or interest.

6. *Depressed children may have a short attention span.* Unlike depressed adults who seem stuck within their dark mood, however, a depressed child can seem suddenly, but only momentarily, relieved of her suffering. She may be able to focus on a problem or a topic or a game for a moment, and then her mind clouds over, burdened with despair.

7. *Some depressed children experience a range of aches and pains, or feign a variety of illnesses or injuries.* A depressed child may want to appear ill so that no one will expect anything of her. She may believe that people will only like her and find her interesting if they feel sorry for her.

Ian, nine, sincerely felt ill or injured when he experienced even the smallest ache or pain. "I just don't feel up to school," he would protest weepily. Time and time again he was taken to be examined by the doctor, and time and time again his parents were told that there was little to be done. Ian felt ill so easily because he judged himself to be ill-equipped to participate in normal school life. "I had to stop my math sheet 'cause I felt so sick," he said. "I couldn't answer the question because I was dizzy."

8. *A depressed child does not want to be herself, but instead would love to be someone else.* One sign of depression is compulsive lying—about one's family, one's social status, one's history. But a more common sign is envy. Children envy their peers when they lack confidence. They cannot do anything, they feel, to be-

come the person they want to be, and so all they can do is wish, day-dream, and envy. In very young children, envy is usually focused on one thing—another child's house, bedroom, new computer, pet, or holiday. If only they had what he has, they may think, they would inspire the love or attention or self-efficacy they long for but do not know how to achieve. Later, between the ages of twelve and fifteen, envy can cause immense suffering. As a child despairs of becoming who she wants to be, she may become obsessed by another child who appears to have "got it together" or "knows what's what" or is "in control."

Fourteen-year-old Amy's description of envy was unforgettable. "It's the most awful feeling—worse than any flu. You feel like puking. Your joints ache. I'm not kidding. It's like being hit right in the solar plexus. But you can't double up. You have to sit there and pretend you don't feel a thing." Anything, she said, could "set her off," and set alight the desire to be someone else. Badly distracted by day-dreams in which she had the qualities and features others had, she had difficulty concentrating on school work. Hence, she performed well below her ability, which made her even more dissatisfied, and more prone to envy.

We can see the sense of powerlessness envy implies. How, Amy wonders, can she begin to become who she wants to be? Amy believes that she herself is locked out of this magical place in which someone can become what she wants. It pains her to see others' happiness because she does not think she can realize any of her own aims—because, given her low self-esteem, she does not think she can effectively work towards her goals.

HOW TO ALLEVIATE DEPRESSION IN CHILDREN

Depression involves hopelessness because it is centered on the assumption that one is helpless. In feeling helpless, without control and without confidence, a child cannot define the problems that confront her. A depressed child cannot think up solutions to her problems; she cannot set goals; she cannot take steps toward attaining those goals; she cannot assess the effectiveness of her own behavior or the consequences of her actions. Without these skills, her low self-esteem will set hard as cement. The most effective way to alleviate a child's depression is not simply to address her feelings, but to teach her how to be effective in her own life. **Our task, as parents, is to help a child discover that she has power: she has the power to learn, to interact with others, to set goals, and to attain goals.** Here are guides for teaching a child the skills that will cut a path through her depression.

1. *Help the child set realistic goals for herself, goals that are appropriate to her abilities.* Extremely high goals, which are impossible to meet, might really be an excuse for not setting herself goals in the here and now. Goals that are too easily met might indicate that she is afraid of a challenge. Some children become depressed because they feel that so much is expected of them, they barely know where to begin. Instead of encouraging her to think about being a Picasso or President or sports star, try to discover what she wants to achieve *today,* or this week.

   This may take a little time, because depressed children have difficulty focusing on what they do want. But such a child can be helped as we make suggestions, and encourage her to make suggestions about how her life could be improved, if only in a small way. She may want to gather the courage to speak to other children, to join a game, to participate in a group project, to learn a new language or a musical instrument. But, at the same time you help her formulate simple and specific goals, try to prevent her from setting herself goals that are so simple that they do not involve any effort at all. If she sets as a "goal" something she already can do, she will not gain any sense of effectiveness from doing it.

2. *Help her work toward those goals.* A reluctance to work toward her goals may indicate a belief that attempts are bound to fail, and therefore that effort is not worthwhile. Depressed children need special emotional support as they begin to learn the skills of self-esteem. We can provide this emotional support by helping her track her effort and her progress. "Were you able to talk to your friend/join a game/help with a project?" we could ask.

If her goals are task oriented (for example, "I want to read an entire book" or "I want to write a full page" or "I want to finish this puzzle" or "I want to shoot one hundred goals"), we can provide a non-distracting environment, following the guidelines already set down for easing anxiety (see pp. 44–55).

3. *Allow her to admit failure, when she has failed, and discuss with her what went wrong.* Instead of trying to boost her spirits by denying that she has failed to progress toward her goal, acknowledge her feelings (with something like, "That must be disappointing") and work with her to discover why she has failed. Make sure that she sees that many reasons for her failure can be changed. Did she fail to make a friend because she gave up too quickly? She could persist another time. Did she fail to volunteer for the school project? She can now understand that it takes more effort than she thought, and be better prepared next time. Was she unable to write the composition/draw the picture/finish the model she wanted? Talk with her about where she got stuck, and how she might get a little further next time.

In gaining confidence she will be able to think more positively about her problems. She may need support in tracking and criticizing her efforts, and assessing how well she is doing. A confident child can admit failure because she is flexible enough to try a different way, and try again to solve a problem and achieve a goal.

4. *Show her that she can safely admire other children's successes— without envy and without making herself seem bad in contrast.* A child with strong self-esteem can take pleasure in other children's skills, talents and characteristics, but a child with low self-esteem feels defeated by other children's abilities. Track the way you yourself note other children's skills/appearance/personalities. Do you note them with anxiety, regret, envy? Try to link up with your child as you admire another so that you will be sharing admiration. Instead of saying, "Why can't you do that, too?" suggest something like, "It's great that she can do that!" Then turn the focus to your own child. This focus could be in the form of offering her a compliment, but it could also be simply a show of attention, which will remind her you find her interesting and significant (for example, by asking her about her plans for the day, or her opinion about an event or even whether she thinks your scarf matches your coat).

5. *Help her make decisions, stick with them, and cope with the consequences.* Some consequences will be good and some will not, but help her learn how to adapt to changes she helps instigate. Decisiveness usually indicates that a child is good at focusing on problems and generating solutions. But depressed children do not trust their feelings or thoughts, and so they need our help in experiencing what it is like to make a decision and keep faith with it. When a child decides she will go to a party, or join a swim team, or sign up for summer camp, or work for a scout badge, or take tennis lessons, then—if she is depressed—she may well need our help banishing doubts about whether she is doing "the right thing," whether she really wants to do what she has decided to do, whether she should really be doing this at all. We can persuade such a child that it is important to follow through

the original plan, see how it works out, and learn more about what she can do and what she likes doing as a result.

6. *Listen to what she says, acknowledge it, and explore her ideas and feelings with her.* Many depressed children feel as though much of their minds and hearts have gone underground, buried by others' disappointment or disapproval. They may be afraid to speak their minds, or may even have lost touch with themselves so they barely know what they want or how they feel. A child may feel constantly irritable, finding fault with everything, and not realize that her "sour" mood is really despair over herself. As we saw with Amy, she was aware of her envy, but not the depressed sense of powerlessness that lay beneath it.

We can retrieve these buried aspects of a child by showing that we want to get to know her, and will not "punish her." When she talks about feeling low or even wanting to die, a parent should avoid saying, "You don't mean that!" Instead, we should explore her feelings. We can ask: What does she want to avoid? What, in particular, is so awful about her daily life? What does she dread in her future? And when she expresses a bleak outlook, we should not be outraged. Instead of exclaiming, "What! I don't believe you said that!" we can offer comfort. A listening parent has enormous power to heal a child because a parent's attention helps focus a child's attention. Instead of feeling shame for her feelings, she will learn that they can be acknowledged— and changed.

A depressed child cannot simply be "cheered up": She needs to be understood and guided. When we work with her to set goals, to make decisions, and to accept failure but to keep going, we will help guide her toward a more positive outlook: She will then experience her ability to be effective and gain confidence. When we listen to her and offer understanding, we heal the shame and ease the isolation that go along with depression. With these guidelines, we can help all children learn how to be effective, how to make careful choices and begin to take responsibility for, and control of, themselves. These are the skills that constitute self-esteem.

In this chapter I have suggested ways in which parents can help their children move from anxiety to control, from anger to acknowledgment, from helplessness to effectiveness. Because anxiety, anger, and depression are such impediments to a child's positive development, however, we have to accept that, if they persist, we may need professional guidance to help our child, or to help ourselves interact more positively with our child. Therapists, counselors, and psychologists may be trained to key into a range of thoughts and feelings that we may not be so adept at handling. A trained outsider, too, may catch patterns of interaction that, in spite of good will and love, are more harmful than helpful.

Later, I will show how parents can extend their support for their child's self-esteem through the ups and downs of school, discipline, friendship, sibling rivalries, and adolescence. Before I go further, however, I want to take time to address problems we may have with our own behavior: For we, too, have problems in managing some of our emotions and solving the problems that confront us. In the next chapter, I deal with the realities of our limitations in self-control and self-management, and suggest ways we can soften the impact of our inevitable imperfections—and actually use these imperfections to extend a child's emotional intelligence.

four

How to Be an Imperfect Parent without Ruining Your Child's Life

I could not have written this book, nor would I have felt moved to, if I did not know what it was like to be impatient with a child who needs my support, or to a find a child's scream of frustration vibrate to the exact pitch of my own, so that I want to scream, too—but louder and longer. I have known the splitting experience of feeling a child's need for understanding and encouragement, and being locked in my own preoccupations. My responses to my children can swing with ease from anger to guilt, from irritation to regret—a pendulum on which many parents ride. Yet, like many other parents, I am often haunted by the idea that an ideal parent is always wise, controlled, and caring, and all too often I believe that only an ideal parent is good enough for my children.

"Current expectations of parents and parenting," writes Janet Walker, "are greater now than at any time in history and meeting them has become increasingly difficult." Is too much now expected of parents?

When today's grandparents were children, their parents probably had firm and fixed ideas of what a good parent did. "Good" parents, in their view, made sure their children were housed, fed, and clean. They would also teach children good manners, and the skills necessary to earn a living or take one's proper place in society. Love was important then, as it is now, but love was seen primarily in terms of responsible, practical care. The current generation of parents is under severe pressure. Good parenting is seen to be essential to raising children who can integrate into family, work, and society. Many of our children's experiences outside the home have to be countered: where they may be exposed to violence, greed, and indolence, we have to teach them respect, restraint, and responsibility. But while we feel a special need to care for the psychological well-being of our children, we also face special difficulties in giving our children the time and attention we believe are necessary. Our lives in the workplace are more demanding than ever. Our jobs are less secure than they were a generation ago. Personal relationships are more complicated and transient. We experience more demands on our time, less control over our future, and increased stress in all aspects of our lives. How, then, can a parent of today be an "ideal" parent, who constantly displays love and patience, who always practices self-control and takes control of a child?

Even as we assume the awesome responsibility of parenthood, we remain people, often stretched beyond our limits. How can people whose lives have ups and downs, who undergo mood swings and changes in fortune, whose most cherished relationships can crack, whose carefully constructed goals can crumble, be good parents? Most child-rearing books tell parents how to be good, better, and best. Such advice can be enormously useful. But as we aim for perfection, we also may need help dealing with our imperfections. In this chapter I show parents how to prevent their own limitations from harming their children, and suggest ways in which these limitations can become sources of a child's crucial emotional education.

The most common parental "faults"—or impediments to parenting according to our best standards—stem from

- anger and stress
- depression or bereavement
- fear, leading to overprotection
- divorce or separation

Some of these parental flaws are linked. When under stress, we are more likely to feel anger, and hence express our frustration and disappointment in potentially destructive ways. Excessive fear—about our children's well-being, their future, and the quality of our relationship with them—may arise from stress, depression, or bereavement. In such circumstances, parents may need special understanding of how a child is likely to respond. In such circumstances, parents may need special guidelines to maintain a positive relationship with a child. The purpose of this chapter is to suggest ways we can remain good parents when our tempers, temperaments, or personal circumstances give us a hard time.

Anger and Stress

Anger is most commonly cited by adults as the source of greatest discontent with themselves as parents. Children list a parent's anger as the thing they fear most in the home. Even moderate displays of anger can overwhelm a child with sadness.

As Dora slammed drawer after drawer of the hall bureau, looking for her daughter Caitlin's gloves, she strung together a series of complaints: "It always has to be at the last minute, doesn't it? Why can't you get ready the night before? I mean, just a little ready. Some things ready. This is stupid, this rushing about in the morning, leaving everything to the last minute." One drawer stuck, and she grunted in frustration. It opened, she found the gloves, handed them to Caitlin, and, from Dora's point of view, the episode was over, a customary blip in family life. Twenty minutes later, however, as Caitlin approached the school gate, I asked her how she felt. "When Mommy's mad a mountain grows in my throat," the six-year-old explained. The "mountain" is that "lump in the throat" we feel when we are sad. This mountainous lump also contained anger—a mountain of words, which she dared not speak, putting a mountainous distance between her and her mother.

Children experience a parent's anger as an immediate, almost physical reality. It changes their environment, and threatens their stability. It makes them sad, and it makes them angry—because it is humiliating, because they feel "unloved" or even, as nine-year-told Lupita said, "ugly." From talking to children about what a parent's anger feels like to them, I was given a clear account of several different ways of experiencing anger:

- For some, anger sweeps around like a tornado, hitting out at everything about them, rather than focusing on a specific trait or complaint. "There isn't one place that's safe. Not one tiny weeny place that doesn't hear him when he shouts," said Grace, eight, of her father's anger.

- There is anger that jabs at a child, or tugs him this way and that, almost like being spun physically around. "It goes on and on, and on and on. And I sort of stand back and watch it coming and coming, but then I have to—well, like wake myself up—because I have to run ahead and say something to stop it," explained ten-year-old Jim.

- Some feel anger like a blast of shame, as though the parent's anger were bound to open an entire criminal file. Nine-year-old Billy explains: "While she's yelling . . . I worry most about what's coming next. Maybe she's found out lots of things, even things I don't remember, so I won't be able to say I didn't do them for sure. So I kind of hold my breath and wait for it to end. Once I asked whether that was all. You know, is it over now? Boy, that got me into trouble."

- Some parental anger makes a child angry herself as she protests against the humiliation. Lisa, fourteen, said of her mother, "When she's angry her eyes are like darts, and you feel she's so full of self-righteousness and you're so full of shit . . . she sort of trembles and you get the feeling that if she had her way, if life was just, you'd be wiped off the face of the earth."

Because a parent's anger can arouse such anxiety, children are likely to develop defenses to protect their self-esteem against it. But these defenses tend to build up false or highly fragile self-esteem. If a child seems to respond to your anger strongly, you may have to protect her from her own defenses against you. Some defenses involve:

- *Deceit:* Children tell lies to avoid being shouted at. For some, this is automatic. "I try not to lie," fourteen-year-old Ellie insisted, "I hate the stories I make up. But when my Dad asks me something, all I think about is what I can say that won't make him shout. It's like you're standing on the edge, and you're about to fall, and you'll say anything not to."

- *Avoidance:* Many children will go to great lengths to avoid a shouting parent. Even if the anger is not directed towards them, they will feel implicated in the angry atmosphere. A child will avoid expressing her thoughts and feelings, and may forego the fun of being with the parent, out of fear that something will trigger the parent's anger.

- *Aggression:* In some children, a parent's anger arouses the desire to strike back. The "lip" or "attitude" with which the child retaliates may lead to an escalation of angry exchanges. Yet most children find shouting at their parents as humiliating as being shouted at. "My voice goes all screechy," twelve-year-old Kathleen said, "but it seems so small, echoing in my ears, but not getting out. And I always cry—that's the worst part of it. I cry these awful big tears, and my nose starts running, and I look so silly."

To save herself this further humiliation, she tried, "to be hard, like [my older brother]. He does a great move with his shoulders—it makes my Dad so angry, but Jim looks so cool, like he can just shove the whole thing out of his way, with the ways he moves his chest." Jim's "hardness," which Kathleen so admires, is another defense. He hopes to humiliate his parents by showing them that their rage has no effect on him. This defense, too, can lead to escalation, as his father may think that he has to shout more to get through to Jim.

Another aggressive defense is to play the clown. Peter, eleven, giggles when his mother shouts—partly out of nervousness, partly to disguise his pain. Kathleen describes the humiliation of allowing her parents to see how upset she is. Jim and Peter defend themselves by hiding behind indifference.

Parental anger can be a very important method of communication. It is not always inappropriate, and in the chapter on discipline, I will discuss the importance of appropriate anger. Being inappropriately angry, too, however, is also an inevitable aspect of being a parent. It is often triggered by our deep involvement with, and investment in, our child. We care so much that we can become badly disappointed or frustrated when our child is not behaving as we think she should. And children can indeed be infuriating. They will do anything to get our attention: they will nag, whine, sulk and storm, rather than be ignored. *But if a child exhibits some of the responses described above—deceit, avoidance, or aggression—we need to work on our anger.*

The first step is to *track* our anger. Are we more-than-normally angry? Is our anger frequently inappropriate to the child's behavior? Questions we can pose to ourselves are:

- Do I shout when a child interrupts my train of thought?
- Am I particularly riled by even minor changes in the domestic schedule?
- Does a child's expression of emotion—either of excitement or distress—arouse extreme irritation?
- Do all a child's requests suddenly seem excessive?
- Do I get very angry at behavior that is really only inconvenient, rather than objectionable?
- Do I frequently shout when helping my child learn something or complete a task?

If the answer to several of these questions is "yes," then stress and anger are interfering with parental empathy, which is the ability to respond positively to a child. Stress can put one in the following frame of mind: "Life is so difficult for me that other people are selfish/thoughtless/wrong to make further demands on me." If a parent feels this way, his reactions to his child may cause her to feel devalued and disempowered, leading to a loss of self-esteem. There are two steps we can take to limit the damage: One is by managing our own anger, and the other is by compensating our child for the anger we cannot manage.

MANAGING OUR ANGER

If our anger or stress is affecting a child, we can take steps to observe, understand, and gain greater control over our own feelings:

- We can observe ourselves to discover whether there are particular times or situations in which we are likely to become angry. Are we more likely to be angry in the morning, under the pressure of getting everyone ready to start the day? Are we more likely to be angry as we prepare dinner, or at bedtime? Are we most angry when we help a child with homework, or when we urge her to practice her music or dance? **By explaining to a child that some situations arouse our anger, we both suggest how she might avoid arousing anger, and show her that our anger is not really directed at her, personally.**

- Once we have worked to become aware ourselves of circumstances in which we are likely to become angry, we will be better equipped to manage our emotions. The "turtle technique" is one good way of avoiding our danger points. This name, used by Jean Gross, makes use of the analogy of a turtle, who draws its head and legs into the shell in time of danger. This involves keeping out of the fray until different ways of handling the situation are envisioned. We can step back, perhaps counting to ten until the pitch of uncontrollable anger has passed. We may decide that we simply cannot engage in discussion while we get ready for school and work in the morning. We can decide that we can only help a child with homework after the supper is prepared. **As we learn to manage our own emotions, we set an important example to our children.**

• We can enlist our children's help: An outburst can be avoided by warning our child that this is not a good time to make requests, to engage in quarrels with siblings, or ask for nonessential help (such as finding school books or items of clothing). We can say, "I do get angry when you refuse to practice. You don't like me to be angry, and neither do I. So can we try to avoid it? This is just something I hope you can do without making a fuss."

Children often enjoy helping parents avoid anger, when they understand how to do it. **This technique encourages children to be more aware of others' emotions and the contexts in which they occur.**

• We can watch what we say, even when we are angry. We can try to be as specific as possible about the object of our anger. The skill we may need to acquire is to both admit we are angry, and limit the scope of anger.

It is far better to say: "I'm angry because we're going to be late," than it is to say, "You always make me late." It is better to say, "I'm angry because you've left your homework until this last minute," than it is to say, "Your attitude toward your homework is awful." It is better to say, "I can't discuss this now—I'll get angry if I do," than it is to say, "Don't keep sneaking up on me with these requests when I'm busy."

If we acknowledge our anger, we may be able to explain to our child precisely what we are angry about. **A child will be far less threatened by anger that is directed toward a specific action than by anger directed towards her general behavior or attitude or motives.**

When we cannot avoid stress and the anger that accompanies it, we may have to compensate for it. We should not compensate by offering money or presents or treats, but we can compensate by highlighting the positive aspects of our feelings toward a child. Here are some simple but effective pointers:

1. *Set aside some quiet time with your child.* Adults cannot always provide the calm security children wish for and to some extent need. Life does not always allow us to be calm and secure; but we can nonetheless remind our children of the solidity and security of their bond with us. As Anne realized that her nine-year-old daughter Becky was becoming more withdrawn, that she tread carefully to avoid arousing her mother's anger (practising the *avoidance* defense), Anne found that Becky's spirits were restored simply by spending half an hour each day alone with her mother. "Sometimes we read, sometimes we bake. Even when we barely talk, there's a sense that we're communicating," Anne noted. This quiet time, which makes a child feel special, also eases her fear of rejection, which is at the basis of a child's terror of parental anger.

2. *Make your positive feelings clear.* Parents can do this easily. Our interest, smiles, and hugs go a long way with our children. They clear the air of anger, which can often hang in the home like stale cooking smells: A child needs to be reminded that your anger does not destroy your good feelings for her.

3. *Give your child opportunities to make decisions.* Usually when one parent is under stress, the entire family becomes more rigid. The child then may feel powerless—and the sense of powerlessness is a trigger for low self-esteem. Allowing a child "say" in some matters can boost morale considerably. The parents of Nick, seven, had been having a rough time in their relationship,

with much shouting and exchanging of accusations. Nick withdrew from all family discussion, until his parents deliberately sought his opinion about what the family might do during the weekend, or what should be on the dinner menu. At first he seemed confused by this invitation to be involved in family life, but rapidly he earned this role, and once again participated in family conversation.

4. *Acknowledge your child's emotions.* In a tense home environment, a child will want either "to let off steam" or to enjoy her own, very different emotional reality. This may irritate a parent who is preoccupied with her own concerns, but it is crucial to acknowledge a child's feelings. When Kathleen shouts (as she becomes aggressive in defense against her father's anger), her father could say, "I see you are as angry as I am." Then her "small voice" would have a hearing, and her frustration would be eased. Such acknowledgment often leads to further communication. As her father takes note of her anger, Kathleen feels both understood and accepted. The power of listening to what a child is saying should never be underestimated.

5. *Let your emotions become a source of understanding.* Since your problems may be an inevitable part of life, a "problem" can be used as a focus of communication and connection. After all, one reason a parent's anger can be so terrifying is that a child does not understand where is it coming from and where it might go. Nick thinks his parents' anger has the potential of exploding the world, and Becky is puzzled because she does not see what causes her mother's anger, and so cannot anticipate it.

It may help if parents talk about their own experience of anger. This introduces a child to discussions about emotions. Billy's mother could say, "When I get angry at something you do, I feel angry about other things you have done, too. Anger, for me, is like that. It's a kind of glue that collects other things with it." If Billy could explain to his mother how frightening he found this, then she could work on controlling certain aspects of her anger. "I'll try to stick to one issue at a time: when you've done something that makes me angry, we'll discuss just that, and try to leave everything else out of the discussion. You can remind me. Okay?" In this way, Billy would gain a greater understanding of anger and see how it might be controlled.

6. *Never deny the anger you actually feel.* If we deny our true feelings, we may "save face" momentarily, but we badly confuse a child. A child with strong self-esteem has a good understanding of others' feelings. A child who sees that a parent is angry, but hears a parent insist, "No, I'm not angry," may come to mistrust her own readings of others' feelings. Children learn to identify their own feelings, in good part, by a parent's own honest identification of feelings.

Using these techniques, we can keep the lines of communication open throughout the whirlwind of our moods. With such reassurance, and respect for her own responses and observations, a child can not only weather parental outbursts, but learn crucial lessons from them.

Parental Depression and Bereavement

"I sometimes feel there's a screen between me and Andy. He's talking to me and asking me to look at something or help him with his homework, and I might as well be watching a kid on television . . . It isn't that I don't want to reach out to him. It's just that something seems to be putting a damper on everything I do—so that by the time I get around to it, he's gone to someone else, or turned away."

—Eva, mother of Andy, eight

"Do you think someone can disappear? No, no, no! I mean disappear and still be there? I like ghosts, but I'm not talking about ghost-things. Yeah. I like ghosts, but lots of my friends think they're scary."

—Andy, son of Eva

In the previous chapter, I spoke about children's depression. Parents, too, can be depressed and, as a result, find special difficulty in engaging positively with a child. Bereavement, or the mourning for someone who has died or left, can have a similar effect: A parent may grieve so deeply, that her love and interest in a child may, for a time, grow dim. To prevent these emotional states from depressing our children's self-esteem, we must understand what they mean to our children and how we might sustain contact—for without positive contact with a parent, a child's self-esteem is greatly at risk.

WHAT IS A PARENT'S DEPRESSION OR BEREAVEMENT TO A CHILD?

Depression is not merely unhappiness: It is a state in which our spirits are low or "depressed," but our responses are also depressed. This means that one is not emotionally available to others, and does not tune in to others' inner states. For friends and colleagues, this can be off-putting. The depressed person seems "cold" or "dull"—no fun to be with. For a child whose parent is depressed, the effect can be devastating. A child needs a parents' full and flexible responses, but a depressed parent does not engage with anyone fully, even a dearly loved child. This can be confusing and distressing—and depressing—to a child.

Andy sees, with remarkable insight, precisely what depression is. The responsive person he knows his mother Eva to be, disappears. She is still present, but an important part of her is not available. He fears that this part of her is dead, and he performs a psychological somersault to protect himself from this fear. He denies that her absence makes her into a ghost—a dead person; but just in case it does, he asserts that he *likes* ghosts. Any mother, however distracted, however "not there," is better than no mother at all. Hence, he will accept her, whatever she is. *He,* after all, does not find ghosts scary, as do his friends.

Bereavement has many of the same symptoms as depression—sadness, sense of loss, diminished interest in people and activities. It can also cause enormous upheaval. The death of a partner will change the entire dynamics of a family's life, both in emotional and practical terms. The death of a child may cause profound personality changes in a parent; and the surviving siblings may be frightened, confused, and (irrationally) guilty, while they also cope with their own grief.

However difficult in their different ways bereavement and depression are, the similarities between them lead me to suggest similar tactics for reducing the effect of these feelings on children.

HOW DOES DEPRESSION OR BEREAVEMENT AFFECT US AS PARENTS?

Bob, father of seven-year-old Tim and nine-year-old Chris, was depressed following a period of unemployment and a series of unsuccessful job interviews. "The kids come home and I can hardly raise my head to say 'hi.' Tim rushes in but Chris pulls him back, and takes him out to play. No one wants to be with me when I'm like this. I try to change. I try to raise my head. I even try to smile. But by the time I've managed to think about this, they're out and away."

Emma felt "too down to laugh" at her seven-year-old's jokes because she was on constant "overdrive." The pressure of work seemed endless, and she could not believe she would "ever have time to be a good mother again. Everything is now on 'automatic,' and there's nothing real going on inside me. I only think about what I have to do. When Steve starts chattering and tapping my back to get my attention, he's knocking at a closed door. I don't know how to respond any more. All I can do is keep running."

Casey, mother of twelve-year-old Dan and fourteen-year-old Derek, felt so drained by the death of her father that even her children "lived on the other side of a bridge, in a land that I can't enter. They may be asking me for something—I know they used to—but I can't key into it now. It's like the thread that holds us is broken. I keep trying to catch hold of it, but I'm not quick enough."

Parents are supposed to be responsive and watchful. The parents' job, we are repeatedly reminded by professional and lay experts on child rearing, is to provide a stable, warm, loving home environment. But parents themselves live in an environment that is often unstable. They often confront severe disappointments. Much of their energy may be drained away by demands in their personal or professional lives. Though they feel the responsibility to set their strong negative feelings aside, they cannot always do this.

PROTECTING OUR CHILD FROM OUR PAIN

We cannot always control depression, and we cannot avoid bereavement. Yet we can take steps to avoid damaging a child as a result of our own suffering. Here are some possible strategies:

1. *Provide your child with other sources of comfort and responsibility.* An unavoidable bout of depression might be a time to en-

courage closeness to another parent or relative, or longer association with friends. A grandparent or aunt or uncle can be a good source of support. Relatives often have resources of feeling that may, in the ordinary course of things, be neglected. A little effort can give a child access to these resources. If the relative does not live nearby, then phone calls and letters can be encouraged.

Even pets can provide good supplements to parental love and attention. Taking care of a pet can make a child feel cared for herself, and the excitement with which some pets greet their people provides enormous satisfaction. A fourteen-year-old said that she felt her cat understood her more completely than any person: "He doesn't judge me, either." Ten-year-old Sara said, "My dog is the only member of my family I like all the time." No pet can substitute for a parent, but the image of the St. Bernard as a nanny in Peter Pan, and the impact that the dog Beethoven had on the family in the film, register the real role a pet can play in providing emotional support.

2. *Never deny your depression.* Often parents feel obliged to deny that they are feeling bad. They may say, "No, I'm not unhappy" in an attempt to protect a child. Such denial, however, can confuse a child. There will be a discrepancy between what the child sees and what the child feels allowed to believe, or what the child knows about you and what the child can talk about with you. Denial of one's feelings does not protect the child from them. A child will feel more protected and secure if feelings and perceptions can be voiced.

3. *Acknowledge your child's feelings.* If you are in mourning, then your child is likely to feel bereaved, too. "You feel very sad. So do I," is actually more comforting than the less plausible comment, "You'll soon get over it." Remember, a child's ability to understand and deal with emotions is far more important than

simply being cheerful. Emotional intelligence, which involves the ability to acknowledge and deal with a wide range of feelings and frustrations, is a key element in self-esteem skills. Parents foster this type of understanding through *emotional coaching,* in which they identify emotions, both in themselves and others. As a child learns to recognize and describe her own feelings, she gains awareness of the situations in which her own emotions arise. She also is then better equipped to see how varied people can be as to what they feel—and when and why.

4. *Show your child that she has the power to comfort you.* This tactic is invaluable: a child hates to feel helpless in the face of a parent's unhappiness, and will gain confidence through the ability to make a parent smile or laugh, or to distract a parent from the "blues." Though you should avoid making your child feel responsible for your moods, though you should not use the child as a dumping ground for your worries, you should acknowledge a child's comforting presence.

Felicity found that even in her darkest moods, she could feel better by sitting on the floor in her eight-year-old son's room. While Imran played with his Lego and train set, or sketched the intricate tanks and airplanes that he was so good at drawing, she would find the rhythm of his activity restful. Maggie enjoyed talking about other things to her eleven-year-old son, even when she was preoccupied by her own grief: "Your ideas are so interesting!" This showed Saul that he had the power to distract her from her unhappiness.

5. *When your mood does lift, share this reprieve with your child.* Depression is usually not permanent, and grief fluctuates in intensity. When we feel better, we should share those feelings with a child. It will be reassuring for the child to know that "blue" moods are not permanent. "I sometimes feel almost happy," can set an important example of resilience to a child.

Fear or Over-Protectiveness

Why is fear seen as a weakness that may threaten our child? Fear for one's child stems from love and concern. Watchfulness, protectiveness, and a keen scent for danger are built in parental behaviors to help infants and children survive. A parent's fear preserves the safety of a child.

Yet a parent's fear can become a child's handicap when it interferes with her confidence to explore and exercise her abilities. In the novel *Other Women,* Lisa Alther realizes that an important skill in parenting is non-interference:

> Hannah saw Mona needed only to realize she was now riding the bike on her own, so she lowered her fingertips and fell back. As their fingertips touched for the last time, and brushed apart, Hannah felt a pang of joy and pride, mixed with anguish—at the loss of the little girl who couldn't ride a bicycle . . . As Mona rode back, her eyes bright with triumph, Hannah first understood that parenting was a series of such small daily deaths, and that learning to let go of your charges was as crucial as learning to take them on.

Forbidding a child to ride a bike, or roller skate, or climb high on a jungle gym, may protect her from a scrape or a tumble, but it also denies her the chance to exercise the competence and care she may in fact have. If we repeatedly drive a child to school, or walk her to a neighborhood friend's house, we may be protecting her, but we are also teaching her to remain dependent. By telling her she is "too little" or "too young," we may be inadvertently telling her that she is incapable, and deny her the pleasure of learning to do things herself—which is precisely what she needs self-esteem for. We need to check our inappropriate fears.

Different parents assess risk and danger differently, and different children do seem subject to different dangers—depending, for example, on whether they live in an area where traffic is heavy or street crime common. Since children are not generally very good at assessing risk (whatever a friend does seems "safe" or "safe enough"), parents need to be cautious. But a child needs to be independent and to feel a parent's encouragement. Nor does a child want to receive the message that she is incapable of acting on her own.

How can we begin to gauge the balance between excessive fear and reasonable caution? Since accidents are always possible, and children are able to get cuts, bruises, broken teeth, and even broken limbs doing almost anything, including playing "quietly" at home, worry about a child's safety always has some rationale. But we need to live our lives with the assumption that normal activities are safe enough. We need to help our children develop confidence. To gauge whether parental fears interfere with the optimism essential to our children's ability to get on with life, here are some questions we should ask ourselves.

- Does every physical activity seem potentially dangerous?
- Am I only *not* worried when my child is at home with me?
- Will an activity be ruled out simply because an accident is possible?
- When I teach my child to swim, or ride a bike, do I feel more worried than my child that something will go wrong?
- When I watch my child on a play structure, do I unnecessarily go to her aid several times at each session?
- Do I worry about her falling long after I know she can walk?

- When she walks home from school, do I routinely worry about her being abducted or hit by a car?

If a parent thinks he is excessively fearful, inhibiting or overprotective, then the best strategy is to enlist the opinion of the second parent. This route allows one parent to air his fear with someone who is equally concerned for the child's well-being. Sharing concern is one of the best checks and balances we have as parents.

But a second parent is not always available, and two parents do not always share the concern a child deserves, and one parent does not always trust the other. In such circumstances, advice from a respected friend, who is also a parent, can be useful and enlightening. Discussion with other parents, who have different experiences of different children, can offer invaluable guidelines as to how to make activities—such as walking home alone, accepting a lift from a friend's older sibling, engaging in a sport, traveling, dating—as safe as possible. But advice and information never provide clear-cut directives. A parent's decision will always be a matter of judgment and of balance.

Our children will be far more likely to find us guilty of excessive caution than they are to appreciate our reasonable care. The best we can do is continue to pit our assessment of danger against our children's need to have their judgment and independence encouraged. In the following section, I discuss ways of getting this balance right.

FEARFUL MESSAGES

In the film *Kramer vs Kramer,* one scene enacts every parent's nightmare. The young boy is playing on a climbing frame while he holds a model airplane. The father sees the danger and warns his son to "Put that thing down," but his responses are slow because he is talking and joking with a friend. His friend—a fellow parent of a playground child—assures him, while they are still conversing, that she will get the toy from the boy. She goes to take it, but before she can grab it from his hand, he falls, and the wing of the plane pierces his face, just beneath his eye.

This scene portrays the close proximity between a child at play and disaster. It shows the ease with which a parent's vigilance is interrupted. It depicts the parent's terror that the worst has happened (has the boy lost his eye?). In short, it underlines our unremitting vulnerability as parents, and the searing guilt when we do not act in time.

What this scene also shows, however, is how the adults' concern makes an accident more likely. The boy is playing happily and confidently on the climbing frame; but when his father distracts him and his father's friend grabs hold of his model plane, he resists the interference, and loses his balance. This scene supports the growing evidence that children perform badly when they sense our fear, and either are infected by that fear, or are distracted by it.

Children have been found to have fewer falls, tumbles, and injuries when they are left alone on a play structure than when parents continually watch them and warn them of dangers or leap to their protection. Children of overprotective parents find it hard to maintain self-esteem because a parent's constant intervention exhibits a lack of trust in the child's competence.

As five-year-old Carrie balances on a high wall, her father yells "Careful!" Carrie stops. The arms that are spread wide to help her balance tilt like a plane in a nose dive. Her pace, previously fluid, stiffens. The pleasure that had lit her face shifts to an amused anxiety. Instead of seeming to say "Look what I'm doing!" her raised eyebrows and open mouth might be uttering the words, "I can't do this—I want to stop." A moment later, as her tense knees buckle, she does stop, using her father's shoulder to help her off the wall.

Carrie would gain in confidence if her father did not express his fear in the midst of her activity. Calls of "Careful!" should be restricted to emergencies. At other times, cautious words should be uttered before or after the activity. If Carrie's father said, "You can walk on the wall, but remember to be careful," Carrie would still be in control of her "adventure."

Children of overprotective parents are frequently clumsy.

As six-year-old Gary swings upside-down, with his legs locked around the metal bar, he has a sixth sense of any danger behind him. His mother calls out "Ooo." He swings far, but not so far as to bang his head on a bar behind him. With a mighty swing, he is upright, and reaching for a higher rung, and his mother laughs. As he loops his knees over it, his mother steps forward to help him. This time, when he swings back, his head clips the frame behind him. He releases his knees, and slips onto the ground.

Gary's parent could refrain both from the admiring noises that might encourage him to do more than he competently can, and from offering help, with its message: "You are in danger" or "You are unable to handle this situation." A neutral eye is the greatest safety valve a parent can offer an active child. Praise can be given, but parental enthusiasm is best given after the activity is completed.

In older children, from the ages of twelve to fifteen, a parent's fear, and the constraints that imposes on them, can become a point of great contention, mostly because a young teenager sees a parent's unnecessary fear as conveying insulting messages about her capacity to be responsible and sensible. In older children, a parent's excessive fear can lead either to **compliance**, in which a child gives up on herself, or to **resistance**, in which case a child can become locked in battle with a parent. But both outcomes can be avoided, or corrected, if we can learn to assess our fears.

Thirteen-year-old Garth responds to parental fear with compliance. His father's persistent questions about whether he could do something convinced him that he could not. Planning to attend a drama workshop on his own, his father asked, "Are you sure you can get there yourself?" and then "What are you going to do if no one shows up?" and "Do you have any idea what that neighborhood is like?" and "Are you sure it isn't going to end too late?" The worry that he could not manage made it all seem unmanageable. "I can't be bothered," he concluded.

Garth backs away from these negatively loaded questions: For his father is not simply asking for information; he presumes that difficulties *will* arise. Garth hears the message: "It's all too complicated and dangerous."

If Garth's father could assess his own fear, he could change his line of questioning. Instead of framing the questions so negatively (Garth's father supposes there will be difficulties), he could simply ask:

"How will you get there?"

"Who else is going?"

"What time will it end?"

These are questions Garth can begin to answer, because they are not already loaded with his father's fear. From there, Garth can discuss with his father whether the circumstances cause difficulty.

Jody is resistant to her mother's excessive fear. Listening to this fourteen-year-old complain about her overprotective parents, we can see where problems arise, and how they could be solved. Jody says,

"I'm never allowed to do anything other kids are allowed to do. Last week I was invited to a party on a river boat ... You should've heard my mother go on about what could happen, how dangerous it was, and 'no way' was I going. You'd think that outside our house there is some wild swamp with goolies popping up behind every tree. Like I wouldn't be able to give the big bad wolf a mouthful, you know? Like I have no judgment, and am really accident-prone—which I'm not. Look—look at my knees. Look at my elbows. Do you see ragged scars? Nope? Me either. And never, not once, have I broken a bone. I know, you know, everyone else knows that all my friends are going to that party and will come back safely. But because one boat she knows about sank, she's sure the one I go on will too, like the jaws of death are just so hungry for me."

By listening to Jody's complaints, we can understand why she is so angry. Not only is she refused permission to go to a party, but she has to deal with the following messages:

- The world is too dangerous to have fun in.
- She is not equipped to defend herself in normal circumstances.
- She has poor judgment.
- She is accident-prone.

If we can identify ourselves as an overprotective parent (or as a parent sometimes prone to unnecessary fear), then it will be much easier to solve this problem, and avoid the *unnecessary* teenage battles and taunts that stem from it. Jody's mother could:

- Discuss the dangers of the outing or activity.
- Consider together with her daughter whether she knows steps to take in an emergency.
- Assess Jody's judgment in a range of situations.
- Assess her overall competence.

The end result may be the same: a parent may still deny her child permission to go to a party on a river boat; but those harmful messages are avoided. Instead of Jody thinking that her mother finds "everything" too dangerous, she may realize that this particular event is unacceptable, but other events will be possible. Instead of Jody thinking her mother believes her to be ignorant or incompetent, Jody sees that her mother is concerned about the general safety of the activity. She learns, too, how she can improve her behavior to convince her mother that she is responsible.

There will always be battles between a child's and a parent's sense of safety and acceptability: But if we have the skills to track our own excessive fears, and if we have the skills to discuss our views with our children, these battles can become sources of understanding and connection.

When Our Marriage Fails, How Can We Avoid Failing Our Children?

Children have a tough time when their parents quarrel, when their parents separate, and when their parents divorce. It is sometimes impossible to salvage a bad marriage, but is it essential to do our best to help our children through the process of its dissolution. Yet parents become so needy themselves during the process of divorce, that they may be ill-equipped to help when their children may need their help most.

Divorce generates confusion, stress, and anxiety. As a family undergoes the process of divorce, both parents and children become more needy and more difficult. A common off-shoot of divorce is the plummeting of children's self-esteem. Many children of divorcing parents lose their motivation to do well in school. Girls under sixteen whose parents divorce run twice the risk of becoming teenage mothers and giving birth to their baby outside marriage, as do girls who continue to live with both their parents. Girls whose parents divorce before they are sixteen are three times more likely to leave home because of disagreements or ill-feeling. Girls whose parents divorce are four times more likely to marry before the age of twenty—probably in the hope of replacing their broken family.

Boys whose parents divorce before the age of sixteen tend to exhibit even more disturbing symptoms of low self-esteem. Incidents of delinquency, truancy, and aggressive behavior are higher among boys whose parents are divorced. Boys hide their pain by being "strong" and "tough" and by inflicting pain on others. They control their sense of loss by feigning a "couldn't care less" attitude. But children whose parents understand them and keep close to them during and after divorce, can be fully protected from such symptoms of low self-esteem.

HOW TO HELP YOUR CHILD COPE WITH DIVORCE

A child of divorcing parents is, like the parents, hurt, angry, and confused. There are no means by which a parent, while terminating a partnership, can prevent a child having these feelings, so such feelings should never be ignored, belittled, or denied. We can, however, cushion these feelings and prevent ill effects.

1. *Encourage your child's continued involvement in school, friends, hobbies, and sports.* Many children feel powerless when their parents divorce. As a child sees that she is unable to assuage either parent's pain or keep her family whole, she may wonder whether she can have any positive influence on the people around her.

   Ron, ten, became aggressive toward other boys when his

parents decided to separate. "Guys I once liked? Yeah, I've whammed them, too. Sometimes you just think: What's the point—you know?—why be nice and stuff, when ... There's just no point."

It is easier to feel his power when he "whams" his friends, than it is when he is "nice and stuff." But if a child can sustain his interest in his own activities and friends, then he has other sources of feedback. He can continue to develop confidence in close relationships.

2. *Absolve your child of guilt for the break-up of your relationships.* Often children suffer enormous confusion as two people they love are set against one another, and as two people they value denigrate one another. Absolve your child of guilt, and offer frequent reminders that she is not responsible for your problems. But even when a child knows that she is not at fault, she may *feel* diminished by it. Some children feel shame when their parents divorce. The shame may stem from the belief that they played some part in the divorce.

Mike, fifteen, concluded that "My Dad left to get away from me and my Mom quarrelling." For some children the low self-esteem that accompanies divorce has a straightforward logic: "My father did not seem to like me enough to stick around," reflected Jose, thirteen.

"It wasn't you—it was the relationship with your mother that I had to leave" may begin to ease this response. You could also talk in some detail about why the marriage did not work. *Avoid, as much as possible, attacks on your partner, and focus on the failure of the relationship, rather than on the faults of either person.* Such explanations will fill in the background to the break-up, and make it more difficult for the child to conclude that it must be her fault.

3. *Show your child respect—for her feelings, her words, her ideas, her*

choices. The care and respect a parent gives a child can go a long way toward easing any shame or humiliation she may feel as a result of the divorce.

Many children feel shame because their unhappiness seems to mark them as "bad" or "odd" or "pitiful." Gail, nine, said, "I'm playing with my friends and I suddenly remember all about Mom and Dad. Then I go all silly because I'm afraid someone will see inside me. I don't want them to . . . I couldn't play with them . . . I don't think I could play with them if they knew about those feelings inside me." Some children cover over the shame they feel with the fantasy that their parents will one day get back together. For most of them, the relentless realization that this will not happen is disappointing and humiliating.

Hannah, eleven, reflected, "I constantly tell Mom she can marry Dad again. Even when he married someone else, I thought, 'Well, he divorced Mom, he can divorce this woman, too, and marry Mom again.' But he has this new baby—this perfect new baby—I guess that means he's never coming back to us?"

Hannah's mother can acknowledge her daughter's feelings: "You feel cast aside by your father's new daughter." Gail's mother can show respect for her daughter's feelings: "I see you often feel that your friends really don't understand what's going on." Such simple acknowledgment often leads to an extended conversation: this may not remove the unhappiness, but it will remove the shame.

4. *Be as trustworthy as possible—on big issues as well as small.* When we divorce, when we form new families, our children may well experience our behavior as a betrayal. It is understandable that they feel this way, and we have to take deliberate steps to counter it. Any promise we make to them should be kept: A broken promise will confirm their sense of betrayal,

while our ability to keep our word will assure them that we can still be trusted.

Try to keep promises about pick-up times, about when you will take a child riding, or skating, or when you will take her to buy new sneakers. Such reliability is extra important when so much of her life is in flux. Your reliability can give her confidence by assuring her that she has a stable place in your life. Above all, keep contact with your child, and allow her access to you if she wants it. This is the best way of showing that you care.

Sometimes parents who do not have custody of their children feel they are unable to offer their children enough to make the contact worthwhile. Some parents feel superfluous, and so step back from the child. Some feel that all they can offer is money and material goods, and hence offer these, but little else. Whenever we participate in the break-up of a family, we must assure our children that we still love them, that we still feel connected to them, and that they still have rights to our time, energy, and resourcefulness.

5. *Do not minimize the downside of a divorce, but highlight what remains the same.* When family life, as a result of divorce, becomes difficult, admit this, but also assure your child that many things are all right. Divorce is not one change, but a series of changes. As a child experiences the range of change in her life, she may feel despair. For Colin, twelve, the harsh financial adjustment became the focus of his grief: "Dad's leaving, so you think, 'Okay Dad's leaving' . . . But there's also all this other mess, about money and stuff, and no way can you do the things boys with their dads at home can do. Sometimes I go to my room and trash it. They've made such a mess of things, and I'm sitting right in the middle of it."

A parent can help ease a child's sense of loss by renewing her appreciation of what they do have. Together they can make lists of all the things they still have. For example: "I still have my health, and my skills and my energy; we still have each other; and you still have your other parent." The activity of making such "still have" lists usually increases a child's sense of closeness to a parent—and that closeness provides the best comfort.

6. *Demonstrate that you can take care of yourself.* For the parent who remains primary caregiver of the child, the most important task is to assure the child that you are all right, and that you can face whatever problems arise. Children have a deep need to see their parents as competent. This parental competence can be as important for sustaining a child's self-esteem as are affection and approval. One of Ruthellen Jossleson's patients explained: "My mother was very warm and loving. With both my parents, there was a lot of physical affection. Lots of hugging and kissing, and my mother always told me how wonderful I was and how much she loved me. But I knew that neither of my parents could solve any problems. *I felt like an orphan.*"

By showing a child that when you have problems you can take steps to remedy them, a child gains confidence from your strength.

Children can survive the uneven patches of temperament and fortune that all parents experience. We can help them tolerate our own inconsistencies, and we can use difficulties to teach them the language of complex emotions. A parent's ability to speak to a child about emotions is related to a child's own ability to understand herself and others. Psychologists now realize just how important emotional intelligence is: An emotional education is every bit as important for life skills as an intellectual one. As we explain why we sometimes feel as we do, and behave as we would rather not, we offer our children perspectives on the adult world. We forge a link between their knowledge of what it is to be themselves—in their child's world—and their perception of the world into which they are maturing. With honest explanations of our own feelings, we add depth to the relationship.

When we break the so-called rules of good parenting—when we fail to stay calm, cool, and in control, when we are unable to provide financial security for our children or maintain domestic stability—we can still be good parents. We can help our children learn skills in emotional problem solving—how to focus on problems and envisage a variety of ways of coping with those problems. We can teach them about communication and closeness, and help them map the complexities of the human world. We can remind them that we should keep caring for one another and for ourselves, even when our personal life is not an unmitigated success. After all, our job is not to provide a perfect environment, but to help our children acquire skills to thrive in an imperfect world.

five

Discipline:
The Delicate
Balance

When parents discipline a child they criticize a child's behavior. If a child hears frequent criticism from someone who matters greatly to her (and a parent always does), then she may come to lose confidence in her impulses and judgment. A child who is constantly criticized by a parent will be *self*-critical.

A child who is never criticized, and never disciplined, however, will not only lack the control necessary to achieving self-esteem, but will also feel that her parent does not care what she does. Caring and criticism, discipline and confidence, go hand-in-hand. Yet a happy joining of our care, on the one hand, and our control on the other, is difficult. Much of our success in disciplining a child depends upon the methods we use, and whether a child can experience our criticism as positive, as showing faith in what she can be, not dislike of who she is.

How, and how often, we discipline children depends on what

we think children are and what we want them to become. If we think they are naturally wild or naughty, we will emphasize control and restraint and exercise authority over them. If we think they have good judgment and a natural inclination to do well, we will encourage them to make their own decisions. If we think their immature minds are incapable of reason, we will issue orders rather than explanations. If we think they are naturally reasonable, we will employ gentle, logical persuasion.

The trouble is children are *all* these things—wild and naughty, reasonable and good, impulsive and impervious to logical argument. So we tend to discipline them in a variety of ways, often unsure about which is most appropriate. In fact, parents have more questions than certainties about discipline. Some questions parents have put to me are highly illuminating. They show that whenever parents discipline a child, they are trying to achieve a very delicate balance between controlling a child and trusting a child. The challenge is how to raise a child without lowering her confidence—how to control and criticize, so that a child experiences a parent's care and faith through the discipline.

When parents speak about disciplining children they frequently raise the following questions:

- *How can I guide and instruct my child without giving her the message that she is unable to think for herself?*

    "I can tell her what's what until I'm blue in the face," Daniel, father of eleven-year-old Audre, reflected, "but unless she's able to see what's right when I'm not there, I haven't managed to teach her anything."

    Daniel understands that discipline is not simply a matter of imposing rules of behavior, it is a way of teaching a child to believe in certain rules and follow these herself.

- *How can I make my child ashamed of what she has done without making her ashamed of herself?*

    "I'm at my wits' end," Marilyn, mother of eight-year-old Ben, admitted. "I just want him to see that certain behavior is shameful—because it's so beneath him."

    Marilyn wants to teach Ben that he is better than his behavior.

- *How can I exercise authority over my child, while giving her confidence in her own judgment?*

    "I get frantic when she just doesn't listen to me and goes her own wild way," explained Helen, mother of ten-year-old Sue. "I have to push hard to get some respect. So sometimes it seems like I don't respect her. But I really do respect the person she's trying to become."

    Helen understands that the aim of discipline is not to prove that a parent is in charge, but to encourage a child to take charge of herself.

- *How can I show a child how careless or thoughtless she is, while assuring her that she is a worthwhile and capable person?*

    "I sometimes want to tear my hair out over that boy," Allen remarked of his fourteen-year-old son. "I'm at him day and night. How can I get him to see his best side?"

    Allen understands that the true aim of discipline is not to make a child concentrate on his faults, but to develop his good points.

These questions that parents have so often put to me show how much they understand the purpose of discipline, while their questions also show how difficult it is for a parent to get the balance of discipline right. A good place to start this balancing act is to bring into focus our goals for a child.

Setting Goals

Usually when we embark on a long-term project, which involves a complex series of tasks, we have some idea what our goals are. We may be sanding down a door so that it will close easily. We may be building our dream house, or constructing a model airplane. As we engage in many of our daily tasks, we have some short-term and some long-term goals in mind. For example, we want to complete a document today and, in the longer run, establish a good name for our firm, or a network of business contacts.

As we discipline our children, we may also be aiming for both short-term and long-term effects. We want a tidy bedroom, an undisturbed dinner, and to leave the house on time: so we insist that a child put her clothes away, or sit up and eat and stop teasing her brother, or dress quickly and get her school books together. But we also have the long-term goals of raising a person who is considerate to others and in control of herself. Here is a list of some long-term goals of discipline that can be forgotten in the heat of the moment:

1. *We want to contribute to the development of internal standards.* This means that we teach a child to judge her behavior herself, and to trust her own judgment. There is little point in doling out punishments while a child behaves badly behind our back. We want to raise a child who is able to decide for herself what to do, and why.

2. *We want to teach the child what is good as well as what is bad.* A child needs to understand that some behavior is unacceptable, but she also has to be able to understand that many different ways of behaving are acceptable. So, instead of focusing solely on what not to do, we have to show her what she should do, and help her envision many routes to positive behavior.

3. *We want to maintain a positive relationship with our child, even as we discipline her.* Our love is the best protection she has when the going gets rough, and we want her to trust that love, so that when she needs it, she can draw upon it.

4. *We want to raise children who have strong self-esteem*—children, in other words, who take responsibility for their behavior and its effect on others.

It is helpful, as we consider these goals, or positive markers in disciplining our children, to consider where discipline is most likely to pose balancing challenges.

We want to assert authority, without becoming involved in a power struggle. When a parent tries to discipline a child by asserting his power, then a child's natural urge to sustain her self-esteem leads to a counter-assertion of her power. Then, to suppress that—if the parent sticks to this strategy—the parent must exert even more power, and so on. What transpires is something like:

PARENT: I forbid you.

CHILD: I'll find some way of getting around you.

PARENT: I'll find stronger ways of controlling you.

CHILD: I'll find more devious/destructive/forceful ways of avoiding your control.

PARENT: Then I'll deny you all your privileges.

CHILD: Then I'll make your life hell.

In this scenario, goals of discipline are obscured by an angry struggle for power. The child, angry and humiliated, wishes to punish the parent by withdrawing her trust and love. There are no more confidences in the kitchen or the den; no more smiles or playful grimaces when meeting coming and going from the bathroom. Requests to set the table or clear the dishes may be met—but with an awful silence. A "bad attitude" or "disrespect" or "sulking" becomes an additional point of contention.

Instead of controlling a child through sheer force of willpower, we want to assert authority through our greater experience and concern, giving the message: "This is not behavior that I believe will improve your well-being." This message links authority to care.

We want to show our strength, without becoming an aggressive or abusive role model. It has been shown that children whose parents punish them by shouting, nagging, criticizing, or hitting are more aggressive than children of parents who use other means to discipline them. Though occasional smacking and shouting have not been shown to do any harm and may be a means of communicating to the child "I have had enough!" the violent parent is likely to raise a violent child.

Any physical assault or violent control angers and humiliates a child. Children whose parents humiliate them are far more likely to be aggressive. Their aggressive behavior makes it more difficult for parents to control them, and so more punishment is inflicted on the child, making the children even more aggressive. A downward spiral of punishment, humiliation, and hostility is something we all wish to avoid.

A parent who is consistent and firm, however, and gives the clear message, "These are the limits," will draw boundaries that give a child important information about acceptable behavior, without inflicting humiliation.

We want our child to heed us, without being afraid of us. Fear of a parent causes a child much suffering. I have heard children describe the knot in the stomach or lump in the throat as, day in and day out, they anxiously watch a parent for signs of anger. Such fear can lead to constant lying (in an effort to appease a parent's anger).

It prevents the open communication that is so useful to a child. If we discipline without aggression or abuse, then we keep the lines of communication open: When a child believes she has a "say," or can enter into a discussion, she will not be seriously afraid.

We want to guide a child's behavior, without creating a home atmosphere in which a child feels humiliated. Constant *negative* remarks—"Stop whining," "Quit making that noise," "Don't be so lazy," "How dare you speak to me like that," "Grow up, why don't you?"—create an uncomfortable atmosphere. Moreover, such negative remarks are counterproductive. They lead to more, rather than less, poor behavior. A child who is constantly told not to cheat, lie, bully, or shout may either feel discouraged by these negative remarks, or get ideas of how to behave from them. A child who hears a parent warn her against cheating on her homework or lying about where she is going, may think: "I guess I'm the sort of person who would do that." Whatever the reason, it has repeatedly been found, that *constant injunctions not to do something often result in a child's doing it.* As a child's behavior gets worse, the scolding, the threats, the yelling, the nagging increase. There is an escalation of a parent's anger and a deterioration of a child's behavior. Instead, we can guide behavior by praising her acceptable behavior. In this way, praise and acceptance can become a more common form of communication than criticism and punishment.

We want to criticize a child's behavior, when necessary, but avoid accusations against the child herself. When people constantly accuse one another of poor behavior and bad intentions, they squeeze out the good feelings between them. When a child feels a parent's disapproval, she can be so hurt that she does not want to hear what the parent is saying. "You're lazy/selfish/useless" is *not* constructive criticism. A child either will defend herself against such criticism by dismissing it or—perhaps worse—will believe it and accept that she is "bad" or "worthless."

It is more effective to set standards by showing faith that our child will meet them, and helping her when she falls short. We can still show our love and approval for some of the things she does (by showing interest, pleasure, amusement), even when she has done many things of which we greatly disapprove.

Setting out these goals, and flashing these warnings, can help focus our thoughts as we discipline a child, but nothing is more useful than simple practical advice that can be used in a variety of situations. In this chapter, I offer a tool kit for discipline: But such a set of tools is best used when parents understand why certain techniques work and why others fail.

Styles of Discipline

Some children are well-controlled and engage in positive behavior. Some children are constantly disruptive and disobedient. Parents often lament the fact that discipline is not having the effect they think it should have. When their efforts do not work, they tend to blame the child. "He doesn't take the slightest notice of what I say"; "My warnings go in one ear and out the other"; "He looks right through me"; "I can shout until I'm hoarse, but what good does it do?"

Are some children simply beyond the reach of a parent's control? Or do some methods of discipline work, while others fail? Does the well-controlled child experience more discipline from her parents than the disruptive child, or does her parent practice a more effective style of discipline?

The fact is that some forms of discipline work, and others don't. Studies conducted over many years show that some types of discipline are more conducive to developing maturity—in terms of self-control, social control and taking responsibility—than others. Here are three different styles of discipline—all of them common, but only one is able to meet the goals I described earlier.

THE AUTHORITARIAN PARENT

What is called *authoritarian* discipline involves a kind of parental dictatorship. Here a parent's word is law—beyond question and with no need for justification. The parent who tells a child "You must do this because I say so," and "You must obey me because I am your parent," may control a child, but she gives the child no understanding of the logic behind the orders. A child's "good" behavior, in such cases, is often motivated by fear or an unthinking obedience. Instead of learning how to make sensible, well-considered decisions, the child learns how to follow orders.

This style of discipline tends to impede the development of maturity. When children of authoritarian parents think about how they should behave, they tend not to think in terms of right and wrong, but in terms of angering or placating an adult. This undermines a child's sense of initiative and confidence—and self-esteem. Hence, children experiencing this style of discipline tend to lack self-control and self-direction; they are often impulsive and unmotivated. They have had no training in making independent decisions and in developing their own judgment.

THE PERMISSIVE PARENT

The *permissive* parent is at the opposite extreme from the authoritarian parent. In fact, many permissive parents are reacting against authoritarian discipline, which, in their view, fails to acknowledge a child's natural good sense. Instead of setting themselves up as "rulers" of the child, permissive parents invite their children to be full participants in decisions about what they should do, how they should behave, and what is best for them. Here the parent declines to issue orders, but solicits a child's opinion. "What do you think you should do?"; "How do you feel about this?"; "What would you like to do?" are questions posed by the permissive parent, who wishes to show that she trusts and respects her child. By giving a child responsibility for her actions and conveying the message that she has sound judgment, the permissive parent hopes to encourage the development of responsibility and judgment.

In spite of its good will and implicit encouragement, this style of discipline does not seem to achieve its aims. By refusing to set down rules, a parent denies a child the opportunity to experience self-control. By declining the role of standard setter, the permissive parent fails to encourage a child to discover her potential. By giving a very young child the power to judge for herself, the permissive parent fails to educate a child's judgment. As a result, the parent who treats a child as an equal raises a child who is underdirected and undermotivated. Strangely, the parent who supplies insufficient control has, in many important respects, the same effect as the authoritarian parent who controls too much. Both the authoritarian and the permissive parent fails to instill consistent and reasonable standards for behavior in their children. In neither of these disciplining contexts does a child learn how her decisions lead to specific consequences for which she must be held accountable: In the authoritarian household, a child learns that punishment comes from being discovered, while in the permissive household, a child believes that no punishment is appropriate. While a child of an authoritarian parent lacks training in making decisions herself, the child of a permissive parent lacks training in assessing and correcting her behavior. *Either* extreme permissiveness *or* extreme control are bad for self-esteem and for the development of self-control.

THE AUTHORITATIVE PARENT

The type of parental discipline that does seem to foster both control and growth best is characterized by parents' use of rules and reasons. This style of discipline is called *authoritative:* A parent asserts authority without being merely authoritarian. The authoritative parent presents rules as principles based upon *reasons.* "You must not do that," and "You must do this," are accompanied, frequently enough, by explanations. Reasons behind the rules are not "Because I say so," but "Because you might get hurt," "because you will annoy other people," "because it will involve too much work for me," or "because it wouldn't be fair to your sister."

Such explanations place the rules within a framework that makes sense to the child, who then learns to think constructively about behavior and its consequences. Such explanations offer a base on which a child's sound judgment can be built. Furthermore, children tend to see parents' efforts to clarify and justify policies as a sign of respect for them. This version of discipline—a clearly defined, structured, and enforced set of demands—is conducive to greater self-esteem. It allows a child to gain confidence by using her own maturing judgment.

Positive Discipline

The most effective style of discipline combines setting down rules and explaining the reasons for those rules. To adopt this style we can start with skills in:

- stating rules positively and clearly
- encouraging a child to follow those rules
- explaining the reasons for those rules
- enforcing rules consistently and logically

STATING THE RULES

The first task of discipline is to **make clear to a child what she is supposed to do.** The more specific the instruction, the better.

Some rules will be universal ("Always wear a helmet when you're on your bike." "Do your homework before watching television."). Some instructions are specific to the occasion. ("Tell your brother you're sorry." "Give your friend back his toy." "Put the jacket you borrowed in its proper place."). Some instructions are somewhere in between. ("Sit up at the dinner table."). Whatever type of rule a parent is stating, the behavior required should be very clear. It is far more effective to say "Put your pens and books away," than "Treat your things with respect"—though each instruction is meant to lead to the same behavior.

Listen to the sound of your own voice as you issue orders or instructions. Some ways of stating instructions are easier to follow than others. No one likes being "ordered around." Do we sound threatening? Do we sound angry already? Haim found that his ten-year-old son became perplexed and hostile when he said, "Put that away," in a tone that carried the message "You haven't done what you should"; but the boy had no problem following instructions when the same instruction was given neutrally, with the message "This is what I'd like you to do now." We want the child to hear the instruction, not the criticism.

Give one instruction or rule at a time. Any child will feel angry and humiliated when adults multiply instructions. Jessica, nine, stomped and screamed when her mother said, "Can you set the table? No—not those knives and forks, the other ones. They have to be washed first. Not that way. Straighten the table cloth. Good. But watch out! It's not centered. That looks sloppy. Can't you be a little more careful?" Yet Jessica was happy to follow instructions and criticisms when she had time to complete one task before going on to the next.

Give warning. "We're leaving in ten minutes" tends to arouse less protest than "We're leaving now." "Tidy your room sometime this weekend," tends to be more acceptable than "Tidy your room this minute." Children feel more stress when they are unable to predict what is happening. An order from the blue can shatter a child's present concentration and sense of control. Even a few minutes' warning can allow her to adjust her concentration and restructure her plans and so find the instruction more acceptable. (Of course a child may try to take advantage of this and extend the warning period. If this happens, then the privilege of being given notice will be withdrawn.)

When possible, allow a child some control over how instructions or rules are carried out. Another way of taking the sting out of issuing orders is to give a child some control over how she is to carry out the order. If she is required to shop for food, she might be allowed to decide which store to shop at. If she is to clear the yard, she can decide on the order in which she does it, or if she has to do her homework she might be able to decide where she wants to do it.

After all, one goal of discipline is to raise children capable of exercising judgment independently from a parent. So even as we lay down rules, we can allow her some control over how she will follow them.

Encouragement is a basic requirement of discipline.

Usually when we think of discipline, we think of negative comments and strict control, such as: "Stop making such a racket," "Do your homework," or "Go to your room—you're grounded." But since the goal of discipline is to raise a child who behaves well, encouraging good behavior is a crucial part of discipline.

We are often inclined to leave a child who is behaving well alone. We say nothing if her homework is done, if her room is tidy, if she is quietly occupied. But just as it is helpful to issue very clear instructions about what a child *should* do, it is enormously effective to issue clear descriptions about what a child is *already* doing that is good or right or appropriate. A child is always moved by a parent's attention and involvement: how unwise to save these only for criticism!

A focused description of good behavior is more effective than gushing praise. "You have organized this room so well! The books are in order, and the pencils are in the desk. It's easy to find things now, isn't it?" is far more informative than "What a good boy you are!"

Involvement and interest can replace praise. The best way of reinforcing positive behavior is to take an interest in what the child is doing. Instead of simply saying, "You're so good," ask "What are you making now? Are you modeling it on something, or just designing as you go along?" or "Can I read your book report? Was the book really that interesting? Where did you find it?" These remarks show respect and interest in a child's activity and can be far more powerful than praise.

When children behave well but do not get the attention all children need, they feel slighted. A child who is naturally shy or withdrawn may require special effort to make a parent's approval felt.

Susannah, twelve, noticed that because she behaved well, she failed to get the attention of her more disruptive brother and sister. "After a while you stop trying—you know, like telling your story at dinner. Because I'll just be interrupted, and—okay—if I complain enough then mom or dad will say 'Let her speak,' but it's like—they're letting me speak . . . it's being polite, not being wrapped up in what I'm saying. So I just let them go on, and sometimes I look at the clock and count the time they don't notice me. When they do, it's only to say, like, well I'm reliable, and good, and so they don't have to worry about me."

Susannah may be less insistent on getting a parent's attention than are her boisterous siblings, but she still needs that attention. "Susannah, I want to know about your day" could be effective, as long as she is then allowed space and time to reply. Children should not have to fight or clown their way to our attention.

Being good, or behaving positively, should be worthwhile—a perk for the child, rather than a burden. A child needs to feel the power of absorbing a parent's attention, of holding a parent's ear and catching a parent's eye, of being seen and noticed. Parents must remember that "easy" children need as much attention as difficult children.

Whenever possible, reward good behavior rather than punish poor behavior. Rewarding a child's positive behavior is far more conducive to self-esteem than is punishment of poor behavior. Sometimes, in trying to correct certain behavior, we may actually be encouraging it: The pleasure a child gets from having the parent pay so much attention to him may far outweigh the discomfort of any scolding. Twelve-year-old Clarence, who comes to infuriating and touching life in Tracy Kidder's book *Among Schoolchildren,* disrupts the class because he cannot get the teacher's interest and involvement by doing work that will impress her: so he acts the clown, the fool, the class idiot, to get the focus that makes him feel real.

Often a child's poor behavior is based upon discouragement. As ten-year-old Pat hears her father complain about the way she left her bike out in the rain to rust, she shouts, "I don't care. I hate you! I hate my bike! I hate myself!" She has become so discouraged that she does not care whether her behavior gets worse and whether her father's anger grows. But as her father shows her how to apply chrome polish, and praises her for her methodical work, she sees that her ability to correct her mistakes is praiseworthy. The encouragement is far more effective than the criticism.

Such encouragement can be minimal—such as sharing with a child the pleasure of her skill. "You did that yourself," or, even better, a detailed description of what she did (such as, "I can see that part must have taken a lot of thought" or "You've arranged your desk so carefully. I can see how the pens are just where you can reach them") is a simple and potentially thrilling reminder to a child of what she has accomplished through her own effort and control. Rewards for positive behavior take many simple forms:

- interest (through watching, asking questions)
- involvement (offering help or making suggestions)
- praise (*describing* good points)
- displays of warmth (smiles, pats, hugs)

With these methods, we can get closer to a child as we discipline her, and our child experiences discipline through encouragement.

Crucial Explanations

The authoritative parent who insists that rules be followed, but who also explains the reasons behind the rules, practices the most effective style of discipline. Explanations are crucial because they give reasons for the rules. When a child understands the reasons behind the rules, she is better equipped to make sound judgments for herself.

Reasons can be roughly grouped into the following:

- behavior will damage or endanger the child herself ("It's too dangerous to play near the building site" or "No, you cannot ride your bike there. The road is too busy.")
- behavior will hurt someone else ("You've made your brother sad. Tell him you're sorry" or "You want to keep playing with him, don't you? Then give your friend back his toy.")
- behavior is not acceptable to the group (family, school or society) to which the child wishes to belong ("We want to be able to see your face and talk to you. So sit up at the dinner table" or "I'm glad you want to come with us. Be ready on time.")

Explanations become an important part of a child's education, not simply about what is right and what is wrong, or what is acceptable and what is not, but also about how her behavior will affect others, and why. When our instructions are backed by reasons, we help a child make sense of good behavior. We help her realize how she affects others. We offer emotional coaching as we help her focus on other people's responses to what she says and does. We then help a child manage her own conduct and take responsibility for her actions.

SNAGS IN THE ARGUMENT

There is a snag here, which any parent with a child over five will have spotted. Once a child learns that reasons lie behind rules and that rules are justified by argument, she will engage in heated arguments *about* rules.

Children learn to argue about rules long before they have any real sense of logical argument. They appeal to principles of fairness and equality long before they have any skill in assessing what is fair or just. "It's not fair," "Why isn't it all right?" "You let my brother do it," seem to trip naturally off the tongues of children. The good work a parent does to explain the logic of rules makes more work for the parent.

Many parents who set out to be authoritative end up being, from time to time, either authoritarian or permissive. "I've heard enough. You can't go, because I say so, and that's that," "I'm not going to argue. This isn't a matter I'm going to discuss," or "This isn't worth the hassle. You can go if you want. Go on, then." Exhausted by argument, we may become more inflexible than we would like or more lenient than we know is wise. Such changes in our discipline style do not provide the peace they are meant to: A child will be confused by the parent's inconsistency, and will put it to the test. "How much more can I get away with?" a child will wonder.

A child asks this through her behavior—by being a nuisance again, by begging, coaxing, whining, stomping, thus causing further upheaval in the household. Robert Walker has recorded the self-aware cunning of children as they go to work on their parents. They boldly describe how they "bug" parents with repeated requests that will prove so annoying that a parent will eventually cave in, just for a moment's peace. In Professor Walker's study, children were quite explicit about their strategies. "You just have to keep saying it," an eleven-year-old told him. "You have to be skilled, and it depends what mood they are in." Another method children described to him is "sweet talk": "I just love you, Dad," or "You're the best Mom in the world," can be either flattering or irritating—but either way, it can wear a parent down.

Being an authoritative parent is not easy. Arguments arise as we argue the case for rules. We get swept away by the argument, which becomes itself something to argue about, and turns into a power struggle. Children may infuriate us by arguing back, by refusing to see a different point of view, by failing to accept the obvious rightness of our argument. We not only are upset that our child wants to spend Halloween in a neighborhood we regard as unsafe, or take a trip with a friend supervised only by a fourteen-year-old brother, or that she wants to buy an expensive computer, we also are upset that she keeps thinking that she is right and we are wrong or "unfair."

A child's skill in argument—a skill taught by good parenting—leads to further argument. When parents and children argue, bad feelings are often elicited. In these whirlwinds, neither parent nor child remains reasonable and calm. As we argue, and our children argue back, and we try to convince them with counterarguments, we may sometimes be tempted into dirty fighting. As our best efforts seem to make things worse, we may hear ourselves say things that we vowed we would never say. As we balance the tenderness of our love against the care that requires toughness, there are a few simple things to keep in mind.

Don't distort—describe. When a child argues her case (in the form: "I want to do this, and your reasons for not letting me aren't good"), parents are frequently (mis)led to distort the child's behavior. Instead of saying, "You're making a thorough nuisance of yourself with this nagging," describe the child's behavior and the situation as clearly as possible, "You have asked me whether you can go to the party. I've told you 'no' and I've explained why. I'd rather not go over this again." In this way, we can take a firm position, without abandoning our reasons.

Don't exaggerate—explain. Sometimes when parents see that

the reasons they are giving do not convince a child, they exaggerate the consequences—for example, by making an activity seem more dangerous than it actually is.

"I'll let you get your way, and you know what will happen? You'll lose the next race and the next, the coach will pull out her support, and you can kiss any sports scholarship good-bye. All the hard work you've done will go down the drain." Here Sherry, thirteen, a top swimmer, wants to spend most of her vacation at a friend's vacation home. Her mother, fearing the loss of her daughter's hard-won swim time, exaggerates the risk she is taking. But Sherry, like any child, will spot the weakness of such exaggeration. ("It won't. You don't know what you're talking about.")

Instead, her mother could go through with her the pros and cons of a decision, and confront Sherry with the real risk (rather than the imagined certainty). Depending on a child's age and the circumstance, a parent then has the choice of letting the child decide and live with the consequences, or taking a firm stand, explaining that she cannot accept the risk the child is willing to take.

Don't ridicule—record. Help a child record the implications of what she is doing. John's nine-year-old son Geoff insists he can go to a football game. It doesn't matter that his father cannot drive him home. He can go by himself. "Oh sure," John says. "You can really find your way yourself. How many bus stops? How many changes?"

Instead of telling Geoff his argument is ridiculous, however, John could help Geoff realize the implications of returning home by himself: the route is complicated; he could do it one day, but only after more experience; it is simply too dangerous to make that journey after dark. In this way, Geoff is still prevented from making his desired outing, but his plan is not ridiculed.

Don't threaten—protect. Threats come in many packages. Both parents and children are ingenious in devising new ways of threatening one another. Children can threaten with further displays of anger and increased disobedience. Parents can withhold love, money, and even food. Since threats imply power, they often lead to counterthreats as each claims to be able to do the other more harm:

"I'm not going," Josie proclaims when she learns her mother wants her to stay with her grandmother while the mother goes on holiday. "You can't make me."

"Don't *you* threaten *me!*" Carol shouts to her daughter. "We'll see what I can make you do!"

Threats frame disciplinary problems in terms of power, and that is not where they belong. Instead, we have to make clear that we are using our power on behalf of our child's well-being. Discipline stems from the need to protect a child, not to prove that we are more powerful. So we keep talking to our child, keep explaining, keep reasoning. There are no short cuts to good discipline. But this hard work is worthwhile, and lays a foundation for raising responsible children.

WAYS TO ENFORCE DISCIPLINE

If we punish a child, we want that punishment to be effective.

Punishment is not a matter of proving how right we are and how wrong a child is. Punishment should not be a form of revenge on the child for disappointing or distressing a parent, nor should it be an attempt, simply, to instill guilt or make a child feel bad. Punishment should be a matter of effectively coaching a child to take responsibility for her decisions, actions, and commitments.

Therefore, we should make sure the child knows what she

has done wrong and what not to do again, and help her work out various ways in which she might avoid doing the same thing again. In this way, we criticize her behavior, but show that we maintain our faith in the child. Moreover, in discussing various ways of avoiding such behavior in the future, children come to see various scenarios and various possible outcomes. This capacity to think up different ways of acting, and to imaginatively consider the consequences, is tremendously important in teaching children problem-solving techniques. It brings into focus the fact that they have a choice, that they can do one thing or another. It also helps them think about choices, and teaches them how choices can be constructed. Within the framework of explaining rules, and giving reasons for behavior, parents have a real opportunity to introduce structured strategies for dealing with their problems. Children as young as six are able to reflect on their behavior in very sophisticated ways. Through our methods of discipline, we can encourage this reflection, which leads to an empowering outcome: *For the child who sees herself as responsible for her own behavior, and as able to control her behavior and influence the world around her, has self-esteem.* Here are the steps we can take to guide this process:

Focus on problematic behavior, not on a problem child. Start with the assumption that a child's poor behavior is a problem that can be solved. Her unacceptable actions are troublesome because they are unworthy of her. Such a problem can be solved because it is not the child who is bad, but the behavior.

Define the problem. Identify what the child has done wrong. Explain it to her, and get her help in the explanation. How did it come about? Who else was involved? How does she now feel about it? Most important of all, make sure she understands how the bad behavior stems from what she did—not what others made her do or what "just happened." Make sure she sees herself as an agent— someone who acted voluntarily and whose actions have consequences. Therefore, we should reject explanations in the form of, "Jed made me do it" or "It's Sara's fault." Instead, ask a child what she *did,* and how she can avoid doing it in the future.

We also have to reject many defenses about motives. "I didn't mean to," Ted, eleven, said when his failure to bring stage props disrupted a class play. "It's not like I *planned* it," Diana, twelve, insisted when she discovered she did not have enough time to finish her homework because she had spent the evening on a computer game. "I didn't do it on purpose," Pat, fourteen, remarked when her father caught her cycling after dark without lights. An effective reply (in some form) is: "I know you didn't mean to behave badly, and I believe that you are sorry, but you still did this. You therefore have to accept the consequences, and you have to take definite steps for this not to happen again."

Form various possible solutions. This exercise is important because it teaches a child how to look at a problem: A problem is something that needs to be solved, and the person with the problem is the one who should come up with possible solutions.

Corrine, eleven, broke a window as she was walking home from school with some friends. She explained to her mother that she "didn't set out to cause trouble" and that the other children wired her up: "It was a sort of dare." She reminds her angry mother, "It's not like I'm always messing up" and claims that her mother is "making a big deal about nothing." Corinne's mother can help her focus on her role in the smashing of the window by asking her how she can avoid such behavior in the future. The guiding questions here are:

- What might you have done to avoid breaking the window at the time?
- Can you imagine circumstances in which it might happen again?
- How would you then ensure that you behave differently?
- How can you make sure this poor behavior does not recur?

Help the child see the "punishment" as a consequence of her behavior. If a child sees that she is making amends for poor behavior, then she sees herself as behaving responsibly, rather than simply being punished. This can take the humiliation out of "punishment," and bring it under a child's own control. If something has been damaged by her, then that thing has to be replaced or mended. If someone's feelings have been hurt, or if someone has been insulted, then she must make amends in some way. If she is disrupting a class or a home or the public peace, then she must find a solution to her problematic behavior so that it will cease and not be repeated.

Make sure the child plans a course of action and follows it. Once the various possible solutions are assessed and one course of action is chosen, the child has to then follow it through. Why go to all the trouble of stating rules, explaining them, identifying poor behavior, envisioning solutions and corrections, yet only half-heartedly see these solutions through?

We want to teach the child to be responsible, and to be responsible she has to track and assess her own behavior.

- Is Ted able to remember his promises to his teacher and classmates now that he has decided to solve the problem by getting up earlier and ticking off a list of things he is supposed to have ready that day?

- Is Diana better at completing her homework now that computer games are banned during the week?
- Is Pat more careful with her bike now that she has agreed to test the lights every Monday?

If not, the process must begin again.

LOVING DISCIPLINE

Children need discipline and control. As parents, we understand the dangers of the child's environment in ways the child does not. We have values and expectations that must be passed on. In fact, children see the restrictions that accompany a parent's high standards for their behavior as stemming from concern and care and involvement. They need our help in gaining the confidence they will only have if they take responsibility for their actions and learn how to solve problems—some of which arise from their bad judgment or poor self-control, and some of which arise through accidents or mishaps.

We sometimes see our children as recalcitrant beings, who are focused on getting their own way, oblivious to other's needs, abilities, budget, or time. But children want our help to be "good." Many children express a painful division about a good and bad self, or a between a superficial and profound self. They engage in bad or silly behavior and want to be saved from it.

Aisha, six, said: "I have these nightmares, yeah, about animals and stuff, and it's so creepy in my room, so I go to my Mom's room and I wake her up and she says, 'Can't you sleep through the night just once?' And I felt—I feel so—*yuck*—,"she grimaced and shivered, "because I'm always the one to wake her and make her do things in the night."

Andrew, eight, was like an observer of his own lack of control:

"We went on this walk I was really cold and I kept saying I want to go back, and my Dad grabbed my arm and said, 'Right! We're going back,' and I felt so sad because—see—they were going to walk up to see the waterfall, but now they weren't. I felt bad because I was so selfish."

Often, when we discipline our children, we forget the voice behind the whining and the wheedling and the tantrum throwing, the voice Aisha and Andrew speak with as they describe their sad sense of being "bad," a sense that shows a desire to be good and an inability to attain this goal alone. Children often feel out of touch with their "goodness," yet passionately believe in its existence. Parents acknowledge their goodness by expecting good behavior from them. Children are thought to hide their naughtiness—which they sometimes do—but we would do well to see, too, how they can hide their goodness. The sixteen-year-old Anne Frank wrote in her *Diary*:

> I've already told you before that I have, as it were, a dual personality. One half embodies my exuberant cheerfulness, making fun of everything, my high-spiritedness, and above all, the way I take everything lightly . . . This side is usually lying in wait and pushes away the other, which is much better, deeper and purer. You must realise that no one knows Anne's better side and that's why most people find me so insufferable . . . My lighter superficial side will always be too quick for the deeper side of me and that's why it will always win.

Too often we work hard telling Aisha and Andrew what they already know: that they are a nuisance, that they are selfish, that they get their way too often. Too often we tell a child that she is shallow or silly or frivolous, when, like Anne Frank, she has a good side, waiting to come out, but fears that her parents will "laugh at me, think I'm ridiculous and sentimental, *not take me seriously.*" As we discipline our children, we are helping them build a bridge between their good inner self and their everyday outer self. When a child acquires skills to be her best self—to control her impulses, to trust her judgment, to develop her talents, to express herself and maintain others' respect—she has self-esteem. As we discipline our children, we work alongside them, not in opposition to them. Our task as parents is to help them acquire skills for being as good as their best self wants to be.

six

Success and Failure at School

In previous chapters I have looked at children primarily in their home environment. This is where the foundations of self-esteem are established. But in the classroom, too, children discover and develop much of their sense of who they are and what they can do. In the fifteen thousand hours children normally spend at school—from the age of five to eighteen—they acquire many of the effective or ineffective beliefs and habits that will shape the ways they meet challenges and interact with other people.

How children learn is far more important than what they are taught. A child's attitude toward learning—specifically, her attitude toward her ability to learn and make use of her knowledge and skills—has far more impact on her confidence and, hence, on her future, than the precise facts she knows. Yet this makes tracking a child's progress at school difficult: It is easier to discover the content of a child's lessons than assess her attitudes toward herself as learner and achiever. In this chapter, I outline the attitudes and beliefs a child needs to develop about herself as she engages with the school curriculum. Since this book is addressed primarily to parents, I suggest ways that parents, too, can teach these crucial lessons.

Learning Goals

Every child has a natural need to think highly of herself. In other words, children need and, indeed, crave self-esteem. For this need to be satisfied, however, a child must believe that she is capable of doing well and succeeding in a variety of ways. But success and failure are not simple measures. They are complex concepts, involving several interrelated attitudes and beliefs. In a good classroom, parents should expect a child to learn four crucial things:

1. She learns that it is important to do well and to learn. I call this *attainment value.*
2. She learns to set and meet *standards of performance.* This means that she develops a concept of what doing well means, and she becomes able to judge how well she is doing.
3. She learns from others what to *expect from herself* and develops *positive beliefs about her abilities.*
4. She also learns that her *effort helps her achieve.* She learns to attribute attainment to effort and persistence.
5. She learns that her performance is important to others. Her individual achievements have *social value.*

Encouraging the Value of Attainment

A child's desire to do well is so natural to her that she will cease to care about her abilities and performance only if she is subject to repeated discouragement. So the guidelines for parents really are meant to prevent discouragement rather than to implant something in a child that is not already there. But at school, with its set tasks and projects, with its competitive grading and constant assessment, a child becomes more self-conscious about her abilities and more anxious about others' judgments. Here are various methods we can adopt to protect our child from experiencing these aspects of school as discouraging.

An important way of sustaining the desire to do well is to concentrate on the task as an interesting or exciting challenge, rather than as a proof of a child's ability.

Most children become extremely anxious when they think they have to prove themselves. They try to avoid challenges in which they will come out "looking bad."

Instead of saying: "Let's see how clever you are at math" or "Let's see how you're getting on in reading" (whereby a child feels that she herself is under scrutiny);

Say: "Why don't you try these math problems" or "See how you do with this book" (whereby a child is given the message that an activity, not an innate ability, is being tried out).

Never make judgments about a child's overall intelligence or ability.

We should avoid labeling our child's abilities ("poor reader" or "slow mathematician" or "too clumsy for sports"). To keep the desire to learn and achieve alive, we should help a child understand how *malleable* her abilities are. This means that she understands that she can increase her abilities and talents through effort.

Instead of saying: "I guess math just isn't your thing" or "You're not a natural reader" (whereby a child supposes that she lacks the ability for these things);

Say: "This seems to be causing you trouble" or "This is difficult, isn't it!" (whereby the child receives the simple and more specific message that the task is problematic).

The second message avoids the implication that her current limitations are permanent; it tells her that her abilities are not set in stone but are capable of expansion and improvement.

When children view intelligence as a malleable quality, their learning goals thrive. Such children believe that when they try, they will be able to do what they could not do before. They tend to maintain persistence in the face of difficulty. But when children believe that their intelligence is what it is, that it will not change, they view effort as "a waste of time."

Encouraging Standards of Performance

It is surprising how often parents want to protect a child from any criticism. They feel anxious that any negative comment on anything a child produces will be unfairly discouraging. Also, parents are biased and may think that everything a child does is "terrific." But such "encouragement" can actually discourage a child. If a child is told that everything she produces is "wonderful," she is discouraged from developing standards of performance. She grows confused about what "doing well" means. Her desire to develop her own critical judgment is frustrated.

Children often work hard to get adults to understand their need for some accurate assessment of their work. By the age of six, they become touchy about others' compliments, especially if these compliments do not mesh with their own hard-earned sense of reality. I was amazed how many quarrels between parents and children were initiated by a child's rejection of a parent's compliment:

Angie, eight, cried in frustration when her father told her she was a "genius." "I feel like a stinky marshmallow when they say things like that," she proclaimed.

A child is frequently confused by excessive praise. Angie wonders what her father means by "genius," whether other people share his view, and what she has to do to maintain his high regard, so the unwarranted praise makes her angry and anxious.

Peter, seven, smashed his clay castle into a heap because he did not agree with his father's assessment that it was "great."

A child hears indiscriminate praise as a dismissal of his genuine efforts to achieve something according to his own standards. Peter chooses to destroy his clay model rather than let it gather undeserved praise.

Julie, nine, rolled rather than skied down the mountain because she disagreed with her parents' praise of her skiing.

A child who hears unrealistic praise feels deprived of motivation to try harder. Julie feels that her father, by praising her skiing, totally ignores the difficulty it presents to her. She refuses to keep trying, because his assessment is, in her view, unrealistic.

These children passionately want to see themselves as smart, creative, and skillful. Like most people, they generally enjoy praise, but they also need to confirm their sense of reality. Angie, Peter, and Julie know they have to improve their skills to be as good as they want to be. They want a parent's help in moving forward, and are disappointed by the parent's attempt to make them content with their current level of ability.

We encourage our children to become positively self-critical by being both approving and accurate. It may sometimes be better to say,

"You've done this well. You can make it even better by working on it," than to exclaim, "That's wonderful!"

As ten-year-old Helen completes a woodwork project at home, she sands the edges, trying to achieve a perfect fit between the lid and bottom of the pencil holder she is making. While she works, her anxiety mounts, and she compares her project to that of a friend, whose design, she believes, is more imaginative, and whose hinges, she says, fit "just right." She fits the hinges on her own box carefully, and sees that it can close properly, but the effect is not what she planned. "It's awful! I've ruined it!" she exclaims. Her face crumbles, and she has difficulty breathing: Her belief in the value of concentration and hard work, her sense of her own worth, all seem poised for a dive.

As her mother empathizes with Helen's frustration, she insists: "It is good. It's perfect!"

"It's not. It's not. It's awful. I can't do anything!" Helen cries.

A better strategy might be for a parent to join in the child's dissatisfaction and to help the child construct that dissatisfaction into a plan for improvement.

"I think it's lovely, and I especially like the way the lid is shaped. Curving it like that must have been difficult! The edges are now so smooth. I understand you want to make it better. What would you like to do?"

In wanting to do more, and in choosing a difficult task, Helen's self-esteem is also being exercised. We should never protect her either from these aims or from her critical frustration by denying her high standards. But we may have to help her define precisely how to meet those standards, and we can ease her anxiety about attaining them by reminding her that she has already achieved something.

The best praise for a child is encouragement of her own good judgment.

Developing a Child's Expectations of Herself

Until the age of four or five, children take for granted that they are who they are and that others are how they ought to be. They may not be happy with the way things are, but they accept them as normal or inevitable. Though younger children also make comparisons between themselves and others, these comparisons tend to be practical and momentary: who gets a place on the parent's lap, whose birthday is coming sooner, who gets the longest cuddle with the puppy, who gets the most attention or approval. But by the age of six or seven, children begin to conceptualize the differences among themselves and to put themselves and others in certain categories. A child now makes new kinds of judgments about herself and others. Some children are better at school. Some are better at sports. Some are quicker to make friends. Some easily gain the approval of adults. The child sees her peers as people who, like herself, are small and dependent, but who are also vastly different from her and in some ways "better," in some ways "worse."

During this phase, as a child develops a strong sense of how much others can do, she may feel that she falls short of her own and others' expectations. *A child needs our special help in making these comparisons safe, especially if she shows at least two of the following tendencies:*

- she is reluctant to admit that something is difficult for her
- she dwells only on far-reaching and far-away goals (such as becoming an Olympic medallist or media star, without actually working toward these goals)
- she speaks disparagingly of all her friends
- she thinks all her friends are better than she at everything
- she loses interest in school

Parents can offer special reassurances in the following ways:

1. *Acknowledge her self-doubt.* Instead of dismissing self-doubt with expressions such as "You can do anything if you try," or "Don't be silly! You can do it!" listen to her fears. Offer support, while registering her fears. "The first day of school can be hard and scary, but there will be other people to help you, and I'll be here at the end of the day to hear all about it." The message is: It is natural that some things will be difficult, but difficulty is not a sign that you are unable to do it.

2. *Set clear and attainable goals.* When a child thinks that all other children outshine her, she may be failing to focus on what she *can* do. One way of getting her to focus on her own abilities is to set goals and watch herself achieve them. For example, you might ask, "How well do you have to do on your history project this term to feel you've done well?" This will help her concentrate on her own work, rather than looking at her friends' work. Or, you could ask, "What *time* do you want to make in the next race?" rather than "What medal do you want to win?" or "Whom do you want to beat?" In our highly competitive culture, we may have to take deliberate steps to remind a child of noncomparative achievement.

3. *Assure her that she is valuable even when she is not a "star."* We can ground a child in the pleasure of making progress, at her

own pace. "See how many more math problems you've got right this week than last" can be more effective than "You're an ace mathematician." "You can now swim a whole lap without stopping," may be a more encouraging comment than, "You'll soon be headed for the Olympics."

A child who is lagging behind her peers will need your support if she is to continue to believe that she has a range of abilities.

• *Find some subject or activity that stimulates her interest.*

Reading may be difficult for her, but perhaps she has an excellent memory. She may have a complex grasp of stories, though find a series of steps in math problematic. Make sure she practices—and improves in—the things she is good at, too.

• *Show your involvement and appreciation of what she can do in these areas.*

Point out how much she is doing well. When a task comes easily to a child, she may not see how difficult it really is. "You remembered there were two uncles. I read you the story, and I'd forgotten that!" or "That was such a detailed description of your outing! I can imagine the bus ride perfectly."

• *Refer frequently to the areas in which her abilities lie.*

The best way of doing this is by showing your awareness of these abilities. "Matthew, do you remember the name of the street?" can be a reminder that he often does remember things others do not. Or "Sam, you're so good at finding things—can you look for the swimming towels?"

• *Insist that she continue to make efforts in subjects or activities that are more difficult.*

If you allow her to concentrate only on the subjects or activities that present her with no problems, then she may learn to avoid the frustration that any challenge involves or assume that you think she cannot succeed in other areas. To forego problematic areas simply because they are problematic, prevents her from learning how to tolerate frustration and work through difficulties.

How a Child Explains Successes and Failures

The way a child explains why she is successful or why she fails is extremely important to her self-esteem. **The reasons a child gives for her successes and failures affect her self-confidence and her motivation.** We constantly tell stories about our successes and failures, even though we may not be aware of it: We account for a success or failure in terms of ability (or lack of it), luck (or lack of it), hard work (or lack of it), outside help (or lack of it). A child's thoughts about what lies behind success or failure shape her beliefs about her self and her expectations for her future. The following example shows how this happens.

Suppose Nancy wants to be an expert basketball player. In particular, she wants to be an expert shooter for her school team. Each day she tries to score thirty baskets in practice. On some days she does this after thirty-six throws of the ball, and some days it takes fifty throws to score thirty goals. In some matches, every shot is a goal, and in some matches she scores nothing.

These fluctuations are part of being human, and therefore not fully predictable. Sometimes the differences will be outside Nancy's control. In some matches she will be playing better teams than in others. Her teammates will also play better on some days than on others. Even when she is practicing by herself, however, using the same ball and the same hoop, she will do better on one day than on another. How she explains these inevitable fluctuations to herself may determine her beliefs about her abilities.

Here is the *constructive* response:

If Nancy sees her best days as proof of her true abilities, and her worse days as a "blip" on the normal curve (a sign, perhaps, that she is not trying as hard as she might, or that she is tired, or has not been eating well) then she will probably see herself as a good player. Seeing herself as a good player, she is likely to summon up greater effort when she is not playing well. She can put forth the effort because she believes it will pay off. After all, she is a good at basketball, and practice will make her better. Sometimes she will be lucky in being placed against less excellent competitors, and sometimes she will be unlucky in playing a team with players better and taller than she is; but whatever the circumstances under which she plays, she will *try* because she believes that she always has a good chance and the her effort will improve her chance of success.

Here is an *counterproductive* response:

If Nancy believes that a good performance is a "fluke" and that her worse days are a measure of her true ability, she will not see herself as a good player. She will feel terribly anxious before each game because she has no idea how she will do. Though she knows she has on other occasions scored many goals, she cannot count on that happening again, because these past good performances were, she believes, simply lucky, and therefore outside of her control. She may practice, but only half-heartedly, because she has little confidence that her effort will lead to an improved performance. If she experiences a series of disappointing games or practices, she is likely to become discouraged.

We can see from Nancy's different possible responses that *success in and of itself cannot fill a child with confidence*. How she views her successes and failures builds or breaks her confidence. There are two different dimensions to the constructive and counterproductive views of "success" and "failure."

1. *The first dimension concerns her control over success or failure.* If a child sees herself as succeeding either because of her ability or because of her effort, then she sees herself as the agent of her success: She is responsible for, and in reasonable control of, her success. And, if she sees a poor game as the result of insufficient practice, then she can work to change it.

    However, suppose a child believes that a success is simply a matter of chance. In this case, she has no control over her success: It just "happened." She has done well, but this good performance is singular—it is not grouped with past successes and, therefore, does not give her self-confidence.

2. *The second dimension of a child's view of her successes and failures concerns stability or instability.* If a child does poorly on an English test and believes that her mark is a result of being stupid, or "no good at English," then the information she has is "stable": Her natural intelligence is not going to change and, therefore, her school performance is not going to improve.

    If she thinks she got a poor mark because she did not read the required text or learn the vocabulary, then the information she has is "unstable": It is possible for her to change. Next time, she can do more preparation, and do better.

    It is important to note that her awareness of possible change does not automatically lead to confidence. If she thinks she got a poor mark because the teacher did not like her, or she was "just unlucky," or the test was unfair, then the information she has is "unstable" in that it can easily change; but she nevertheless has no control over changing it, since "luck" and the teacher's bias, have nothing to do with her.

A child needs to see two very different things as she assesses her abilities and performance: She needs to see that her ability can change—for both better and for worse—and she needs to see that she has some control over her ability. In the following ways, we can work with a child to encourage a constructive response to both success and failure.

Talk about why she did well. Help a child understand reasons for success and failure. Understanding reasons for successes are as important as understanding reasons for failure. If a child believes that she did well on a math test because she was "lucky," then she will not have confidence in her ability. So, if she does do well, point out *what* she did well ("You understood this complicated problem" or "You were careful and accurate.")

On the other hand, if a child thinks she did well because she is inherently smart or talented, she may think that effort is unnecessary. The confidence that natural ability alone is all one needs can be counterproductive. Remind her that she was well-prepared, or that she had reviewed the material thoroughly, or that she had worked consistently. *Children who believe that effort in school is more important than ability, tend to do much better than children who believe that ability is more important than effort.*

Make sure a child understands how her effort contributed to her success. (For example, a parent could say, "I'm glad you did well—you certainly worked hard on that," "I'm so glad you were able to concentrate during the test," or "That studying sure paid off.")

Discuss what a child might do to change the outcome when she does not do well. You can listen to a child as she blames a teacher, and offer emotional support ("That must be disappointing for you"), but then go on to ask the crucial question: "What can you do about it?" If she has done poorly on a test, go through it with her. ("This kind of problem seems tricky. Let's practice these!" or "When there are a lot of these questions, you seem to lose concentration. Take your time, and see if that helps.")

Such comments focus on the task, rather than the child's overall ability. They send the message that her ability can improve. The message to get across is: "You have some control over the outcome."

The Social Value of Attainment

As important as it is to encourage a child to set her own standards and to judge her work for herself, it is also important for her to understand that the people around her value her effort and achievement and that her abilities have wide-ranging use in her community.

Here are some simple ways of doing this:

1. *Show your pleasure in her effort and her achievement—not only through praise, but also by taking an interest.* It will please a child far more for you to read her composition and remark on it ("That's an interesting idea about the Roman army" or "Let me read this again, more carefully. Your descriptions are so vivid!") than to call it "good" or "wonderful."

2. *Show the her good work has a positive effect.* By saying, "Your report makes me want to read the book, too," a child will learn that she has the power to influence others' views.

3. *Encourage her to pass on the skills she has acquired to others.* "Your brother is doing the math problems you did last year.

Can you help him?" or "Your sister needs ideas for her essay. Could you talk to her about it?"

4. *Encourage a child to do at least some of her school work in a group.* As children work together on projects, each member of the team gains confidence when an idea she proposes is used. A child who contributes to a group experiences the social value of her effort, imagination, and abilities.

Maintaining Confidence in the Classroom

Children's lives at school offer endless possibilities for being found to be "bad," "inept," or "stupid." In her novel *Foxfire,* Joyce Carol Oates gives a vivid account of a fear all children will recognize, and which may jog parents' memories of their own lives as children in a classroom:

> You'd have thought, wouldn't you, that Rita O'Hagan's teachers would have been protective of her, and maybe some of them were, but there was Mrs. Donnehower in eighth grade English who spoke in a bemused patient voice to Rita when it was her turn to read aloud . . . and Rita stammered and blushed and lost her way though moving her forefinger with fanatic precision beneath the lines of print; and there were numerous episodes of humiliation in gym class from which that teacher did not trouble to spare her, poor Rita with jiggling breasts and hips amid a little group of overweight or myopic or ill coordinated girls barely tolerated by the rest; and worst of all was ninth grade math where Mr. Buttinger's drawling nasal voice rang out repeatedly, "Rita! Ri-ta! Go to the blackboard please and show us how it's done!" and the class sniggered in anticipation as Rita fumbled even taking the piece of chalk

from Mr. Buttinger's fingers and went to the board in a daze of in-comprehension and mute physical shame. Not that Rita O'Hagan was the slowest and stupidest pupil in Mr. Buttinger's class (though for amusement's sake she could be made to appear so) but rather that she was the pupil most humbled by her mistakes, most apologetic, most likely to burst into tears.

Rita's paralysis as she is unable to do what her teacher asks, is a fear that stalks every child who has entered the realm of school, grades, and testing. If a child is lucky enough to escape such em-barrassment herself, she will witness another child's humiliation and be anxious that one day she will be in a similar situation. Or, she may be uncomfortable with her participation in the audience that inflicts such pain. The seemingly imperturbable Gore Vidal re-vealed that he continues to dream today about being a child at school and walking, unprepared, into a classroom to take an ex-amination he is bound to fail.

In young children's conversation, too, there are many refer-ences to the shame of being "told off" in front of a class, or being made to feel stupid and, therefore, shamed, isolated, and rejected. Children live with the daily risk of being shamed by their own in-adequacy. Like Rita's teachers, whom one would expect to be kind (and maybe some were), adults often forget what a powerful force this fear exerts. And, as we can see in Rita's case, it is not enough that some adults are kind, for a few unkind adults can overturn the careful buffering of many others. Rita's inability to read out loud in the classroom spreads like an ink blot on wet paper. In feeling a failure in one area, she becomes a failure in many. A mental block leads to physical awkwardness: she is not only unable to under-stand ninth grade math, she also fumbles in taking the chalk from her teacher's fingers. The shame of her failure colors her entire self-image.

Humiliation can inflict a stinging blow to a child's emerging sense of worth. Ann Epstein, a child psychiatrist at Harvard Medical School, says that "One of the most common triggers of suicide in children and teens is a humiliating experience . . . A child's self image is forming continually, and is very shaky. They tend to blow some things out of all proportion . . . So the idea of getting caught doing something bad, in the child's mind, may mean to them that they will always be seen as bad, or if they are embarrassed, that they'll never attain their dignity again. . . . These injuries to self esteem, in their minds, can come to define their whole identity."

The sting of shame can lead a child to concentrate on disguising rather than overcoming her inadequacy. Mark, eight, who had difficulty reading, watched the lips of other children, and fake-read, a half-second behind the good readers. His mental energy went into decoding the messages on other children's lips, rather than into decoding the printed words on the page. Parents and teachers have to catch such children out—not to shame them, but to teach them. A child must come out of hiding and suffer an initial humiliation if he is to experience success.

The child who experiences failure as shameful feels something like this: "This is the sort of thing that happens to me and I am the sort of person this thing happens to." Such experiences can reshape a child's past and future. Old disappointments burn into her anew, and she anticipates future failures. Humiliation, however awful, is felt to be "right" or "appropriate." She expects it, and therefore cannot avoid it.

We, as parents, can help a child overcome this all-too-common experience in the following ways:

1. *Identify the problem that makes humiliation possible.* Find out what "inadequacy" is targeted and describe it as specifically as possible. "It seems that you are embarrassed when you make mistakes reading out loud in front of the class." In this description, the focus is very clear, and greatly minimizes the embarrassment. When a child hears such a description, she is likely to think, "Well, that isn't so bad after all." The "spread" of humiliation is halted: It is merely her reading out loud—not her general intelligence, not her overall reading ability—that is problematic.

   The insistence on identifying the problem will also prevent her hiding it and disguising it. If a child refuses to acknowledge the problem, then she is unlikely to solve it.

2. *Teach your child the difference between mistakes and failure.* As you work with her to alleviate the inadequacy that gives rise to humiliation, make sure she understands the difference between making a mistake and failing. In listening to her read aloud at home, you could show her how her mistakes give important information that can help her solve her problem. "It seems as though you skip over words as you rush to finish," can indicate that mistakes are not shameful, but worthy of attention, and this can be supported with, "That's something that we can work on."

   Remember, Rita is not the one who makes the most mistakes, but the one who is "most humbled" by the mistakes she makes. It could give a child a boost of self-confidence to remind her, "You get lots of things right even if you make mistakes. Everyone makes mistakes. It's part of learning." The message then is: There is no reason to be ashamed of your mistakes. As educational psychologist John Holt writes in *How Children Fail:* "Life holds many more defeats than victories for all of us." We therefore have to teach children how to deal with failure if we are to teach them how to succeed. Though we should try to avoid feeding children an unbroken diet of failure, what we have to do really is to reconceive failure: "we should see that failure is honourable and constructive, rather than humiliating."

3. *Coach her to resist humiliation.* A child who can identify her strengths and weaknesses is equipped to resist humiliation. If she has the capacity to work hard and seek solutions to classroom problems, she will not feel shamed by her mistakes. If a child has the confidence to say in class, "Yes, this is hard for me, but I am trying and improving," then she can rapidly clear the air of embarrassment.

4. *Elicit help from the teacher.* Learning and humiliation cannot coexist. Any teacher who is humiliating a child should be confronted with this problem. A parent may formulate the problem in this way: "My child is having a difficult time. Sometimes the atmosphere makes her too anxious to do herself justice." Such a formulation is more likely to be heard than anything involving an accusation (such as, "You are humiliating my child"). You can suggest that you and the teacher discuss ways of removing anxiety from the learning process.

With these tactics, we can help a child tackle anxiety about schoolwork and provide her with the skills to resist humiliation. We can make sure our child is not the one "most humbled by her mistakes, most apologetic, most likely to burst into tears." Instead, we can help a child be unafraid to try and sometimes fail, because failure is part of learning. The ability to tolerate frustration and to take appropriate steps toward working through the frustrating problem abolishes humiliation and restores confidence.

Dealing with Rejection

In the film *Baby Boom,* there is a scene in which mothers sit beside a sandpit while their toddlers play. They scour their children's diaries for an afternoon that is free. Each day is taken up with gymnastics or drama or pre-school prep or—not surprisingly—a session with a psychologist. The high-powered businesswoman (played by Diane Keaton) who finds her career threatened by the demands of raising a child, discovers that child-rearing is itself big business, as much of a rat-race as her life in the office. These professional mothers arouse her anxiety as they discuss the "necessity" of early training for the "best" schools. What will become of the child in her care as a result of her ignorance? How will her child survive a less than superior nursery school education?

The scene, of course, is a comic exposé of parental ambition. It *is* funny that some parents pour so much energy into a competition that common sense tells us must be unnecessary. Though we may, while watching the film, enjoy a comic distance from those mothers who construct a rat race out of the games of childhood, the reality of competition, cannot, for most parents and children, be denied.

Entrance applications and interviews are usually associated with late adolescence—with college and schools of further education. But a reality of our life is that for many children and parents, these applications and entrance assessments begin at an early age. Parents may believe they suffer most as they see their child denied entrance to a school they believe is just perfect for her—but we should be sensitive to the effect this has on a child.

Self-esteem is closely linked both to a sense of achievement and to a sense of acceptance. Hence, a rejection of this kind can be difficult to cope with. Some children, and some parents, take a rejected application easily, but others do not. Here are some danger signals or indications that the child is responding more negatively than necessary to such a disappointment:

- unwillingness to pursue any challenging activity, even those that were once a pleasure
- anxiety about small mishaps—such as losing things, or spilling something, or missing a phone call
- regressive behavior that lasts more than a week, such as intense play with dolls or soft toys or construction toys meant for younger children
- desire to spend a lot of time alone

A parent can do a lot to restore a child's confidence:

- remind her that disappointment is an inevitable part of life
- remind her that every situation has problems
- talk about your own past failures and disappointments, and how you overcome them (often parents hide their own failures from their children, in order to assure a child about parental strength)
- point out good things about the present situation (this is more effective that than reminding them how bad things might be)
- help her become engaged in her immediate surroundings—with friends, with after-school activities, with homework.
- talk to the child about her past—this helps her build up her sense of having a significant history with many ups and downs; it also provides reminders of the depth of the child's experience and the range of meanings life offers.
- don't banish any mention of the disappointment—this may be an important event in a child's life and should be acknowledged.
- don't allow the child to lower her expectations—such rejections cannot be seen as providing any real information about her long-term success.

Exceptional Children

The ability to *try*—to put forth effort—is one of the most important aspects of achievement and one of the most important building blocks of self-esteem. As a child learns that her own efforts affect her achievement, then her motivation and self-confidence grow. But some children try and try without making progress. They are taught alongside other children, they study alongside them, but the efforts that work for so many other children, fail them.

Increasingly, educators and parents are learning to identify a wide range of differences in the processes and rates of children's learning. It has recently been estimated that as many as 26% of school children are learning disabled—which often means simply that the more common methods of teaching do not work for them, and other channels to learning must be found. Some children have a minor brain dysfunction, which may set up a barrier to learning, yet beyond that barrier lies a wealth of ability. Many learning disabled children have specific "blind spots," which do nothing to diminish their general intelligence. Some children confuse words that, to them, sound similar. Some children read fluently, but writing defeats them, either because they cannot spell, because they cannot coordinate their writing movements, or because they have difficulty holding ideas in their memory long enough for them to be transferred to paper. Some children can take in information that is given to them verbally, while some can make sense of what they see enacted or illustrated, but find it difficult to follow a complex set of written or verbal instructions. Other children can read and understand a story, but then find no way of holding what they understood in their short-term memory—and so cannot take notes or discuss the story. And for some children who have excellent verbal and reading skills, the symbols of mathematics form a non-sensical and terrifying system of signs. They may confuse the word "three" with a different number, or be unable to visualize the symbol and, as a result, be unable to extract the sense of a mathematical question from what they hear. Some children are mildly retarded, but educable, which means that their potential for learning and personal development is considerable.

These special difficulties are so emotionally laden that they can lead to a cruel impairment of self-esteem. Children with special problems can all too easily see themselves as "stupid" or different, in a shameful and humiliating way. *Whereas children with physical disabilities usually cope increasingly well as they mature, children who do not learn in "normal" or expected ways tend to cope less well with their problems as they mature.* If we do not correct a child's counterproductive responses to learning difficulties, then she will believe that failure is inevitable, that she lacks the power to overcome her disability, and that effort is pointless.

How Parents Can Help a Special Child Thrive

Sometimes effort has to be reconceived, just as do success and failure. Different kinds of effort may be necessary. Different skills in trying have to be learned. Special work has to be done to make sure the child has constructive ways of accounting for both success and failure. Each child, whatever her abilities, has a right to an appropriate education. Each child's special disability should be identified and explained, and a program of learning established to meet individual needs. Only if realistic standards of performance are set can such children sustain what all children need:

- attainment value, or the knowledge that it is important to do well and to learn the ability to set and meet standards
- positive beliefs about abilities and realistic but strong expectations of herself
- awareness that effort leads to achievement
- belief that performance is important to others or that her achievements have social value

When a child's learning disability is pronounced, and extensive, the context of success may have to change radically, but a child's need for self-esteem is the same and the techniques for achieving it are the same. Many parents whose children have a mental handicap find that their children far outstrip them in their ability to connect effort with achievement, to be propelled by determination and hope, and to link their ambitions with their efforts.

"I watch Petra work at her drawing. She holds onto that crayon for dear life and marks that paper. She's awkward, sure, but somehow so careful. She gets real engrossed, and the drool starts running down her chin because her tongue is making an effort, too. You have to think, What a great kid. What a winner!" Many parents spoke of the ways in which their disabled children have taught *them* about setting and attaining goals, and putting forth one's best effort.

The most difficult decision for some parents is whether to put a child in a special class or a special school to provide the teaching they need. When children are excluded from mainstream schools and classes, they may indeed feel a blow to self-esteem. The rationale of being held back a year is that a child has another chance to learn what she did not learn, to mature, to "catch up." If a child is taken out of mainstream classes, and put into a special program or class or school, the rationale is that the teaching will be more at-tuned to her level. There is a danger, however, that the negative self-image that can result from these policies promotes such de-spair that they cannot be educationally effective.

The advantage of a special class or a special school is that a child's problems in learning are no longer unusual. She will no longer be criticized for not learning as others do, and the empha-sis will be on finding ways she *can* learn.

As in so many aspects of parenting and teaching, the answer involves a delicate balance of both costs and benefits. Whatever our individual decision, these guidelines will help the outcome:

1. *Locate as precisely as possible the nature of the learning difficulty.*
Some schools provide testing by educational psychologists, but many children go undiagnosed until very late, and con-cerned parents who do not feel the school is sufficiently focused on their child may be advised to invest in private testing. Sonja was furious when her son Ned was diagnosed as dyslexic at the age of twelve. "Do you have any idea how many times we shouted at him to get down to work because the teachers were saying he was lazy? When I think of what we thought, because we thought his teachers knew what they were saying—. I just feel sick. Here's this guy who's really been trying hard, and everyone around him—including me—has been telling him it's all his fault, when the problem is that he really sees things in dif-ferent ways. So all we've been doing is hammering in ordinary ways of teaching him. What a waste of time! What a cruel waste!"

Children like Ned benefit enormously from an early diag-nosis, which then pinpoints the problem, and avoids counter-productive accusations of "laziness." These children can often stay in mainstream schooling with some individual tuition by teachers trained to deal with these highly specific problems.

2. *Remind the child that everyone is good at some things and has difficulty doing others, and that, in this way, she is not different from others.*

A child who does not learn in the way most of her classmates learn is likely to feel "odd" and "worse" than others. If she can get the message that intelligence is *multidimensional,* that everyone finds some things easy and some things difficult, then she does not have to feel that her difference from her classmates makes her "worse" or, overall, less able. Yet she will also have to understand that to acquire some important skills, she may have to work harder, seek more help, and tolerate more frustration than her classmates. This special difficulty can be conceived as a positive challenge.

3. *To emphasize the message that she has true abilities, find something the child really loves to do, and make sure that some time each week is spent on it.*

Marcus, eleven, loved horseback riding, which did involve setting challenges and acquiring skills; but Mike, eight, preferred simply looking after rabbits and guinea pigs. (Children with learning difficulties often have strong responses to animals, and contact with animals can be immensely supportive.) This watching can lead to learning about animals' behavior and needs. Confidence in one area does not automatically lift a child's overall confidence, but it helps a child experience the connections between effort and attainment.

Connie, nine, found doing mental arithmetic difficult: The numbers she heard were not linked to the numbers whose symbols she could sometimes recognize, and each numerical task had to be put to her in a variety of ways before she understood what was required. But she had a lively "literary" mind. She loved words and images. Her teachers and parents were charmed by her imagination, and as the lead in a school play, she gave an assured performance. "There's this difference— yeah?—between doing what I can do, and, well, trying to do things I can't. When I can do something—oh, it's so fun. But sometimes someone's trying to teach me, and my mind's like a tiny pocket of nothing. I don't think anyone who doesn't have this trouble can know what it's like. But you just have to hope that something some teacher says is finally going to help you understand."

With the support of her mother and teacher, Connie discovered the joy of a competent performance. But just as important was her ability to acknowledge her limitations without shame, and to realize that she had to tolerate a special frustration.

4. *Make sure the child understands precisely what is expected of her.*

Any child is likely to be frustrated by not understanding what is expected, but a child who finds learning problematic will be additionally, and unnecessarily, burdened by such confusion. When a child is reading something for a report, explain that she will have to remember some of the material in order to write it down. When she is looking at examples of math problems, explain that she will have to work out other problems on her own. Help her structure her work and her time. "Take notes when you read. Do this by writing one sentence after each paragraph. If you can't do that, I'll help you."

Teachers should also help clarify the number of steps involved in each task. They should structure material so that the children in the class understand the point of the lesson and what they are expected to achieve. They should be willing to repeat instructions or information: Children often need repetition to understand, to check on the meaning or instructions. Teachers should be very clear when they give information and instructions. *Clarity is important in reducing anxiety and confusion.*

5. *Track a child's progress.*

Progress may be so slow that it is not apparent without deliberate comparisons between "then" and "now." You might make a tape of your child reading and then, when you think some progress has been made, play that tape back to her, so that she can see the progress herself. Perhaps you can keep old papers or worksheets, and use them as points of comparison. You can also help a child see the difference between her work when she really tries and when she doesn't. Or, you might compare performances when she is able to work in a quiet room, without being rushed, or without other children working alongside her. If these external factors—noise, hurry, competition—impede her work, then it will be useful for her to know this. "I can do it if I get to do it in the den," ten-year-old Lisane told her teacher. "I didn't do well this week, because I tried to study for the test in the kitchen." She had learned that when she was alone, her slow pace did not make her anxious, and she could learn her spelling. This knowledge gives her greater control over her performance, and thus she is motivated to seek solutions to her learning problems.

6. *Prevent learning difficulties from turning into behavioral ones.*

This is not always easy because learning difficulties may give rise to frustration and shame, and hence to behavioral problems. Tracy Kidder, in *Among Schoolchildren,* notes how easy it is for a humiliated child to become a disruptive child. Other children are quick to understand this. Judy says of her classmate Clarence, "He doesn't understand the work, and he hides behind the things he does, to make himself funny . . ." Clarence uses every ineffective strategy described in this book for evading effort and disguising his sense of what he cannot do. His teacher recognizes this: "There was a deep intelligence in Clarence. But it had been directed mainly towards the arts of escape and evasion and sentry duty."

Educational psychologists repeatedly find that when children with learning difficulties have support at home, they are far more likely to thrive. With the concerned attention of a parent, children are less likely to be caught in a downward spiral in which they play the clown to hide their ignorance and avoid the lessons that might lead to knowledge. If the above steps are followed—if the problem is defined, if the child is assured that she has significant abilities and that with help and effort she can acquire others—then her learning difficulties will not become behavioral ones. As Joy Pollock and Elisabeth Waller remark on the basis of their extensive experience with dyslexic children, a child with help and hope is usually very willing to work hard.

Whatever a child's abilities, we cannot simply tell her to feel proud: Instead, we have to teach her how to earn pride. We cannot urge a child to respect herself with "positive self-talk" alone; we have to help her set and meet standards for her behavior and achievement. A child who sets standards, who works to attain them, who links her successes to her efforts and sees their social value, will have positive resources for self-esteem.

Children's views of their successes and failures grow far more complex as they mature. In this chapter, I have looked at the ways in which children of widely varying abilities can respond positively to the competition that arises at school and gain confidence in their capacity to try and to learn, whatever their natural abilities may be. In the next two chapters I look at competition and cooperation and their effects on self-esteem in very different contexts—among siblings and among friends.

seven

Sibling Rivalry: How Does It Affect Self-Esteem?

Parents try to tell a child that she is loved, that she is admired, that she is as good as anyone. Then the child's older brother says, not just once, but day in and day out, "You're stupid. You're pathetic. You can't do *anything.*" The parents' carefully assembled support is hammered to smithereens.

As a baby, my youngest daughter watched her older sister with an intensity that would have softened the most indifferent heart. This older child was wonderful. She had magical skills. She could tie her own shoes, shout at her mother, skip rope with her friends. When the younger sister was old enough to play, it was always the big sister who decided what game it would be, and who took which role. Whenever the younger came up with an idea, it was judged to be "thick." Toys newly purchased were declared by the older sister to be "too good" for the younger child to touch.

It was not that the older child did not love her little sister. She was amusing, she was even edible—fun to hug, squeeze, and bite; but she was little, not large in significance; cute, not clever; a sidekick, not a leader, and unworthy of the admiration she seemed to arouse so easily in others. So when, at the age of four, the younger sister drew a wonderful picture of her cat, with soft tufts of fur in its ears, and black spots carefully recorded, just as they appeared on the real cat's pink nose, and announced that she wanted to show this work of art to her sister, my heart stopped. Hoping to warn her against the sisterly abuse I knew would follow, I searched for some words of caution. She caught my gaze, and held it solemnly as she explained, "I want to hear her say it's *dumb*. Then I can thump her, really hard."

Why, I wondered, was such fighting necessary? Did I not love them both enough, and give each enough attention, and praise each equally, and show even-handedness in the distribution of treats and favors? Did I not do my best to make sure there was nothing to fight about, no reason to denigrate the other with words like "thick" and "dumb"? But fight they did, crossing the border between horseplay and abuse several times each day. They teased and ridiculed one another, and found one another's successes hard to enjoy and irresistible to undermine.

Many parents feel similar exasperation and despair in dealing with sibling quarrels. "Why can't you let your brother have the ball for a while?" or "Why do you always have to tease her?" or "Why can't you be just a tiny little bit nicer to him?" are common pleas of parents watching siblings interact with one another. Why is such behavior so common among siblings?

In this chapter, I look at the complicated world of sibling relationships and ask: How can parents smooth troubled sibling relationships? How can we encourage the enormous potential these relationships have for the development of love and understanding so that, instead of diminishing a child's self-esteem, these relationships will support it?

How Rivalry Begins

Rivalry between siblings stems primarily from competition for a parent's love. Children fight for parental attention and approval. Why, a child may wonder, when my parents have me, do they want (to have or watch or listen to) another child: Am I not enough?

Sisters and brothers also fight for their position relative to one another. They often really do not want an equal share of family resources, but the largest—maybe even the *only* share. They also want their siblings to acknowledge this power and to give them approval and recognition. Arguments about "fairness" are usually only a front. Complaints such as "She got a bigger piece than me," "You let him stay out that late when he was my age," "You never feel that sorry for me when I'm ill", or "I bet I won't get as many presents on my birthday," frequently disguise the desire to have everything, not just their "fair share" of it. Children learn to argue about a fair division of love and privileges and favors because parents try to be fair and answer arguments about fairness. But parents should never underestimate what a child wants: A child wants everything.

And because a child wants to be served dessert first, and be first to learn how to use the new video, because she wants any birthday celebration to be hers, rather than a sister's or brother's, her sense of "fairness" is never satisfied. However fair parents try to be in doling out to each child equal amounts of attention and love and approval, children themselves see parents as showing favoritism. But though our children are likely to accuse us unfairly of preferring one sister or brother to another, we should not simply dismiss their accusations. Each child needs to be a kind of "favorite." Each needs to feel our special love.

The Danger of Comparing Siblings

For most parents, a child's sense of being less loved, or less favored than a sibling, is nonsensical. Most parents believe they love their children equally. Unfortunately, we can all too easily and unwittingly aggravate the competitiveness that sisters and brothers naturally feel for one another.

As we watch our children with enormous interest, we tend to compare them to the other children we know best—usually our other children. Joshri, mother of seven-year-old Mirfet, said, "I watch her grow—so quick and so graceful—and I know she can do anything. She is like her oldest sister, with her talent and her intelligence. Yes, I do expect much of her, because I know what her sister achieved."

Parents with two children of the same sex have a particular tendency to compare the siblings. They puzzle over differences, and worry that one is not on the same track as the other—or perhaps they worry that the other *is* following the same path. In the television show *South Central,* Joan worries that her son Andre will be killed in a drug gang war, just as her son Marcus was. Sometimes she responds to him as though he were Marcus, and once she even calls him by his dead brother's name, forgetting that they are different people.

Even an only child can experience such intimate comparisons. Tony, twelve believed his father admired a neighbor's son in a way that slighted him: "He's always saying, 'Watch how he pitches that ball.' " RuthAnn, eight, knew that her cousin's chess prize nagged at her mother: "I can't give her anything to boast about."

It is important for a child to learn to tolerate praise of other children, but they also need to feel a parent's attention focused, often enough, on "just them." Children need to develop according to their own highly individual impulses and abilities. They need flexibility, not rigid labels. A child will feel shortchanged and cheated of a parent's true attention if she is put into a slot, or identified in relation to a sibling. Here are some ways parents make comparisons between siblings. We can learn to spot them: Some of these practices we can then avoid; some we cannot avoid, and therefore we need to minimize their effects:

- *A parent may make comparisons as we ask one child to follow another's example.*

    "Why can't you sit up straight like your sister?" "Look at Gemma. She comes home and starts her homework right away whether I'm here to tell her or not." "Even your baby brother is more responsible than you." "You're messier than your two-year-old sister."

    Over time, and used persistently, such comparisons can make a child feel like she is an overall disappointment. "I feel like I'm in the wrong family," twelve-year-old Drake declared. "All I'm supposed to do is be like the others—but I'm just not."

    As his mother cited his sisters as standards by which to measure his own behavior, Drake heard the message: "You're not what you should be, because you're not like them."

- *A parent may praise one child in contrast to another.*

    "I can always depend on you. You're so sensible, unlike your sisters."

    This remark is a compliment, and might be expected to boost a child's self-esteem. But for nine-year-old Tashi, such compliments put pressure on her. "My sisters are so funny, and I wish I could goof around like they do. But Mom needs me to be dependable." When I asked her whether she would like sometimes not to be so dependable, the color in her face heightened, and she look close to tears. "Well—I—you know, maybe. Because sometimes when Mom talks about me—well, I feel queasy. Well, you see, sometimes it makes me angry. But—I just am—dependable. I mean, that's me. Isn't it?"

The praise confuses and angers her: She hears the message, "You don't have the freedom your sisters have."

• *Sometimes a parent has different expectations of his children, which imply very different attitudes toward them.*

Though it is often realistic to praise different levels of achievement in different children, low expectations of one child make her feel less favored. A child may hear the message: "What's good for you isn't good enough for your brother."

Saskia was pleased that her parents did not make her work as hard at math as her brother did, but she also registered the demeaning implication, "It doesn't matter about me," noted this nine-year-old girl, "because I can't—you see, even if I tried, I guess they think I wouldn't be that much better. So it doesn't matter so much."

• *Some (contrasting) comparisons among siblings stem from expectations based on gender.*

"Amy can go shopping, but Geoff and I will go for a hike."

Even as parents tend to be on guard against gender bias, even as we try to avoid assumptions about what a girl can and cannot do just because she is a girl, or what a boy is supposed to be because he is a boy, our awareness of these differences sometimes enforces these gender differences. Many parents learn that they cannot expect their seven-year-old son to sit as long and as quietly as their nine-year-old daughter. Many parents discover that a daughter prefers shopping to hiking. But if we assume that Amy wants to do one thing, and Geoff another, simply because one is a girl and one is a boy, then a child hears the message: "I shouldn't like doing the same things my sister likes doing, because I'm a boy."

If we curtail these comparisons, we have a better chance of giving a child the fine-tuned attention she needs to shape her own identity. We can then begin to address the paradox that "children are what they are," while parents have enormous influence on what children become.

Guidelines for Minimizing Sibling Comparisons:

Focus on the individual child. When watching a child's efforts, successes and failures, try to ask, "What is this particular child trying to do?" rather than, "Is this child doing what her sister or brother did at that age?"

When Patrick stopped insisting that his eight-year-old son was simply lazy because he was not as active as his older brother, did not want to go on frequent outings or play outdoor games, he came to see that his son's "inactivity" was really a kind of reflectiveness. "He sits for hours on a Saturday, and then suddenly draws this lovely thing. When you watch him, his 'laziness' begins to make sense."

Practice noncomparative descriptions. Children are often uneasy hearing that they are better or worse than a sibling. Jacki, whose parents told her she was the "smart one in the family" worried what would happen to her parents' opinion of her if they should realize that some of her friends were smarter, while Stan worried he could not be a doctor because his father thought "he wasn't as smart as Jane." Tashi worried that if she ceased being "the reliable one" in the family, her parents would be disappointed in her.

Practice describing a child without comparing her to anyone. Instead of saying, "You're more musical than your sister"; *say,*

"Your piano playing is going really well. I can hear the nice rhythm in that piece.

Instead of saying, "Look at your brother. He can teach you how to score more goals"; *say,* "I like playing football with you. You're a good team player."

Emphasize the pleasure of an activity or skill for its own sake. When comparisons are constantly brought in, some children think there is no point to doing something if they cannot do it better than their siblings. Eric thought swimming was about racing his brother. Nell thought there was no point to ice skating because her sister was a whiz at it and she was not. Her mother was able to urge her on with, "It's fun. It's good exercise, and we can all go together. Let's just see what you can do." She then confirmed her attitude by giving Nell's effort on the ice as much attention as the older girl's excellence.

Allow each child time to develop her own individual process of learning and thinking and responding. It can be frustrating to have to spend more time with one child than with another, but instead of saying "Hazel could walk to school by herself when she was your age. Why can't you?" or "Why do you always forget what I tell you? Your brother doesn't," explore the child's individual needs. "Why is walking to school still a problem for you? I think you're old enough to go by yourself. Do you want more help crossing the streets? Or is it something else?" and "How can we make sure you remember what I've told you in the morning? Shall I write it down, so you know where I'll be, and when you need to be home?"

Accept that the same treatment for each child is not always right or fair. Different children have different needs. Some children do require more attention. It may therefore be unfair to treat different children in exactly the same way or expect the same things from them. You may have to work with your children to help them understand these different needs, reminding them that difference does not mean that one is "better" or "smarter" than another. "Everyone is different, and you don't want to be just like your brother anyway" is a strong reminder to a child that your different treatment of a sib actually is a way of acknowledging her specialness.

Accept that your child cannot be your version of "the perfect child." When parents have children they are obliged to do the best by the children they have. Sometimes a child is very different from what the parents expected. When Dympna and Stu had a child with spina bifida, they were shocked. "You can reason and reason these feelings away, but they're still there—that there's something wrong with you and you deserve it, or that it's so unfair—just so unfair that everyone else has a perfect child, and you don't." Most people, when thinking about the children they will have, imagine a perfect child. When they have an "imperfect" child, or a child different from the normal one they expected, they have to struggle to give up what some psychiatrists call "the ghost of the perfect child."

All parents have to reshape early expectations as they get to know the real child. In some cases, adapting to the actual child is sheer enjoyment. In others, it involves hard work, while a host of expectations are restructured. But whether or not parents are lucky with a child's "fit" into their family's expectations, this fit has to be achieved. That is the bargain we make with our children. *All* children want to be loved, listened to, and appreciated for who they are.

Expect differences. Get used to the fact that children will be individuals. Children are remarkably different from birth. Some children are adaptable, easily soothed, fall quickly into a deep sleep, like lots of cuddles and attention. Some children are by temperament sensitive to the slightest noise or made easily anxious when their routine is disturbed. Some children are more shy than others, some more fearful, some more aggressive and active.

But children's temperaments are not simply "there"; they are described and given meaning. If we describe them by comparing one child's temperament to a sibling's, we may imply that one of those children is "better" or "worse"; but if we focus on the individual traits of an individual child, we support and confirm her special identity.

Effects of Birth Order on Siblings

"As an older sister myself," writes Judith Viorst, "I will concede that firstborns tend to get the best of things, but they also, I'm certain, tend to get the worst too." Viorst acknowledges that firstborns experience a time of being loved as the only child—which is what every child wants. But because of this "privileged" position, they may also carry a special burden as a result of a parent's high expectations.

Where a child comes in the birth order—whether she is the youngest, the oldest, or flanked by younger and older siblings—profoundly influences her experience. But no position is in itself better or worse. However, there are certain things parents can look out for as they fine-tune their sympathies for their different children.

OLDER SIBLINGS

Possible perks:

- Older siblings tend to have more power, having got a head start in growth and strength and knowledge.
- Older siblings tend to feel greater pressure from a parent's wishes and fears: They are more likely to be ambitious.

Possible drawbacks:

- They are often blamed for the antics they find irresistible because they are seen by parents as being the stronger child, the one more capable of control, the one who carries more responsibility.
- They often feel guilt for the treatment they dole out, swinging from anger, irritation, and the desire to push a sibling away, on the one hand, and regret for what they have done and empathy for the sibling on the other.
- Younger siblings can be an awful source of embarrassment to an older brother or sister—as embarrassing as parents are to a teenager.

To minimize these drawbacks, a parent can:

- Acknowledge her "weaker" or more vulnerable side. For example: "I'd like you to have a place on my lap, too."
- Avoid giving her excessive responsibility, but show appreciation when she does look after a younger child. For example: "Did she wear you out the way she wears me out! She looks very happy."
- Show that you see how the younger child can get the better of her to make her "look bad." For example: "She really knows how to get you angry, doesn't she."
- Ensure some "noninterference" time. For example, tell the younger sibling, "When she has a friend around, we all have to leave them alone."

YOUNGER SIBLINGS

Possible perks:

- Younger siblings can use their less dominant position to gain help from parents. By being "weaker," they elicit a parent's help during quarrels.

- Younger siblings may have the advantage of having parents who are "broken in," or who have learned how to be patient with, less fearful than, or more tolerant of their children.

Possible drawbacks:

- Younger siblings can feel overwhelmed by older siblings' authority and capacity, and may despair of attaining excellence themselves.
- They may get caught in their dependent roles.

To minimize these drawbacks a parent can:

- Give the youngest child special control over certain things. For example: "Elsa chooses the menu/video/game on Friday night, and once she decides, that's that."
- Give the children equal responsibility. For example: "The kitchen needs to be thoroughly clean. Shaun can't dry the glasses yet, but he can inspect them."

MIDDLE CHILDREN

Possible perks:

- They have the advantage of never feeling "dethroned," as an oldest child does, yet enjoying a "head start" on younger brothers or sisters.
- Middle children often become good compromisers and negotiators. They have, after all, experience of two aspects of siblings positions, being both younger and older.

Possible drawbacks:

- Middle children often feel they are neither one thing nor the other: the older and the younger siblings seem more clearly defined.

- As well as feeling undefined, they often complain that the attention allotted to them is tiny, compared to "the high achieving oldest" or the "dependent youngest."

To minimize these drawbacks a parent can:

- Make a special effort to listen to her thoughts and hopes. Focused attention makes a child feel more clearly defined. For example: "I really want to hear what you thought of the film."
- Note their special position in the family. For example: "I think you can understand your little sister and your big brother best of all, because you know what it's like to be both a younger and an older child."

TWINS

Possible perks:

- Twins get special attention. They are head-turners: People notice the double cuteness—two babies in a stroller, two toddlers into mischief, two fetchingly matched children setting off for school.
- Twins play together much more often than other siblings. They also watch one another and mimic one another, and they do develop a closeness that can give a sense of social or emotional protection. Camilla felt that without her twin brother she might be alone, and eight-year-old Chris said that being a twin made him feel "special, and, like, it's harder for anyone to mess with us, because there's two of us."

Possible drawbacks:

- Some twins feel that as a twin, they are less than whole. One may feel she is a shadow version of the "better" twin.
- Some twins develop an exclusively close bond, shutting out other

brothers and sisters and even parents. They then deprive themselves of a wider exposure to people.

To minimize these drawbacks a parent can:

- Take extra care to give noncomparative descriptions of their character and activities.
- Encourage different friends and some separate activities.
- Make sure you spend personal time with each twin separately.

Keeping the Peace

Parents may work to prevent some of the rivalries that emerge between their children; but how can we prevent siblings themselves from engaging in those heated debates about who gets more and who is better? How can we handle sibling quarrels without favoring one child over another?

Brothers and sisters have special difficulty dealing with quarrels because these quarrels tend to have many dimensions. When siblings fight, parents should be aware of how many different issues may be involved. If only one issue is addressed, the quarrel will not be put to rest. Here are some common issues in brother/sister fights:

1. *The "inciting incident" or immediate cause of the trouble.* They may be fighting over the use of a pen set or Gameboy, or privacy and the right to have a bedroom to themselves, or they may be trying to join a sister's or brother's game.
2. *The struggle for power within the family.* Each child wants to have influence in the family—to have a "say" in what she does, to have her belongings respected as *hers,* to have her parents protect her right to privacy or her right not to be verbally abused

or her right not to be hit. When brothers and sisters quarrel, they often want to test a parent to see which child the parent will protect or "side with."

3. *The anger toward a brother or sister that stems from a wide range of experiences.* Brothers and sisters have long-standing relationships, which often give rise to a host of past complaints. A brother who thinks that his sister is more likely to get good grades or win sporting trophies may be more likely to get very angry when they quarrel over something else—such as who gets which place in the car, or who gets first go with the new computer game. A sister who feels constantly excluded from her brother's fascinating games will fight hard to keep her new crayons to herself.

For step-brothers and sisters, quarrels have a somewhat different configuration, with some similarities, and some differences. Step-siblings may have to share family space and parental time, but do not always share a history and the bonding of memories. Their struggle for status may less well-padded by the love and mutual regard other siblings usually share. For step-siblings, the accumulation of complaints about who is favored may be replaced by the accumulation of anxiety and resentment about changes in the family (the death of a parent or divorce and subsequent remarriage). As with other sisters or brothers, the conflict between step-siblings can become an enormous source of conflict for the entire family, as the parents wonder what sufferings and failings—either their own or their child's—underlie the conflict. But the strategies we use to calm quarrels between step-siblings are the same as those we should use between biological brothers and sisters.

And what are these strategies? What can parents do, given that the quarrels are likely to be complicated? If a parent sides with one child, then the other will feel (unfairly) powerful while the other feels (unfairly) slighted. If parents interfere, they may be adding to the grudges that so easily accumulate between brothers and sisters. The best strategy is to guide the children to solve their own problems. Here are ways of helping our children deal with their own quarrels:

Identify the immediate cause of the quarrel. First help them define the issue. Do both children want one toy? Does one child want to set up the train set on her own? Is one child messing up the other's game? Is one invading another's privacy? Is one teasing or taunting another?

Seek their suggestions for solving the specific problems. Once the issue is defined, you can enlist your children's help in proposing solutions to the problem. However, they may need to be persuaded that it is in their interests to negotiate (rather than just insist on having their own way). You could try saying, "If the toy/computer/video is going to be used at all, then you have to decide who uses it first."

Once they understand that their life will be better if they solve the problem, you can give them some instruction about how to come to an agreement. There has to be "give" and "take" in these solutions (otherwise one child feels weak and the other strong, and this relative inequality gives rise to further hostility). You might ask, "Can you agree not to bother your sister when she has a friend? If you can do that, then there should be a time when you want to be alone, and she agrees not to bother you." In this way, the child who has to "keep out" does not lose face and is not labeled a "nuisance" because his sister has to reciprocate by keeping out of his way.

Parents can let the children form their own "contract." Their brief is simply to make sure that both children agree to the solution (who goes first, and for how long, or who keeps out of whose way at what time) and that there will be no further arguing about this same issue. In this way, each child is given responsibility for keeping the (temporary) peace.

View all children involved in a quarrel as equally responsible. Parents sometimes come to the aid of one child more frequently because they see her sibling as the stronger child. But if you are coming to the aid of one child frequently, then there is a fair chance that the child you are helping has set you up.

Alex, seven, and Tim, five, rarely fought (beyond modest bickering) when their parents were busy elsewhere, but when a parent was at hand, Tim would routinely annoy his brother. He would mark his drawing, take a train off its track after Alex had set it in motion, put on his brother's jacket or his shoes and march around, clowning, as he wore them. He paid no attention to Alex's warnings that he was in "trouble." Alex's "Stop!" had no influence on Tim's behavior, nor did it help to pull the drawing away or put the train back on the track. Tim would stop hassling his brother only when Alex jumped on him and punched him. Then Tim cried loud and long, and sobbed quietly in a parent's arms as Alex was scolded. In this case, as in many others between siblings, the inciting incident is an excuse to test one's power with the parents. Alex feels that his parents are suspicious of his strength, and Tim is learning the bad habit of using his "weakness" to manipulate other people.

If we assume each child has equal responsibility for the quarrel, then we avoid favoritism in the following ways:

- We will avoid insulting one by helping her and giving her the message: "You are the weaker one."
- We will avoid giving a child the message, "If your brother hits you, I'll be nice to you and shout at him."

- We avoid giving a child the message, "I care more about your brother's distress than yours."

Be as fair as you can to each child, but remember that this fairness will be for your own peace of mind. Never assume that your children are going to endorse your sense of fairness, so avoid getting trapped into arguments about fairness. Be fair, but do not argue about fairness. In the heated atmosphere of a sibling quarrel, the fine points of others' different needs will not be appreciated. Arguments about fairness will distract from the main goal, which is to solve the current problem. Here are some guidelines for meeting reasonable standards of fairness:

- Avoid taking sides and making judgments—this is bound to seem unfair, to ruffle feelings further—if only by having one child grin and declare, "See, Mom's on my side."
- Address the different emotions that have been aroused by the point at issue: "Sandra, you're feeling that David is preventing you from talking on the phone, and David is worried that he won't get a chance to call his friend until it's too late. Is there some way you both can sort this out?"

In this way, each child is seen to have a legitimate grievance. The message is: "I believe in you both." The follow-up message is: "It is up to both of you to solve this problem."

Tolerate a range of feelings toward a sister or brother. Rosa, eight, was happy to make her brother cry by snatching his favorite toys or blankets from him, by beating him at races, by telling him off; but when Rosa's father shouted at her little brother, she would run to comfort him, and would not leave him until she was able to make him laugh. She needs to let both these feelings have free play. If she is made to feel ashamed of her negative feelings, they may seem more damaging than they really are.

When a child exclaims, "I hate my brother," you might simply nod and say, "He must make you very angry sometimes" (rather than "You don't mean that" or "I don't want to hear this"). In this way, the child is not ashamed of her feelings, nor does she feel she has said something about her permanent attitude toward her brother.

We can listen to a child's anger without sharing it. "You sound really angry now," we could say to a child who declares that she hates her sister. "This quarrel has deeply upset you," we could say to a child who declares she will never speak to her brother again. In this way, we acknowledge a child's feelings, we show we are listening, we offer understanding—though not agreement.

When a child is in danger of being physically hurt, interfere immediately! Though you show respect for a child's feelings, you do not have to accept her behavior. Hitting, punching, and kicking are not to be tolerated. So if there is physical violence of any kind, the noninterference rule has to be ignored! There is nothing more humiliating for a child than to see that her parents do not mind her being hit or kicked or punched. Not only does the victim of physical force feel humiliated, but the child who hits feels ashamed, regretful, and humiliated.

Even while you interfere, however, show them that you have faith in both of them to solve the problem. Help them define and then address the problem while insisting that they find a solution other than physically fighting. You might say, "I know you're angry. I know you're upset. But you'll have to find some other way of showing it."

Make use of the positive feelings brothers and sisters have for each other. As a child teases, taunts, denigrates, or attacks a sibling she loves, as she is rejected by a sibling whose regard she values, her own sense of self-worth is endangered. Good sibling relationships have been found to be correlated with less anxiety in children, and higher self-esteem—not only in childhood, but well into early adulthood. The closeness of siblings, who know the rhythm of one another's enthusiasms and anxieties, who share memories, who help one another find their way through the maze of family interactions, can create a bond unrivalled by any other.

Encourage close sibling relationships by talking to a child about the feelings of a brother or sister. This can start early—even when one child is an infant: "She's crying. She must be hungry. She's looking at you, wondering 'Who's that big child?' " It can continue throughout childhood: For example, "Vic does like teasing you, doesn't he? Why do you think he has so much fun with you?" or "What do you think your sister makes of that interesting game?" Such conversations involve emotional coaching as they prod one child to consider a sister's or brother's thoughts and feelings. This emotional coaching has been found to increase the closeness and understanding of siblings.

Sisters and brothers learn an enormous amount about love and hostility from one another. They can make use of the resources of this relationship best when they feel secure in a parent's love. The key to maintaining a child's confidence in the course of sibling rivalries is to offer her a special love that is for her alone. We can never say too often: "You are each my favorite."

eight

Gaining Confidence with Friends

F riends are extremely important to a child's development and self-esteem. Within her immediate family the child learns many things about her own significance and her potential for relating to others; but it is with friends that she learns about herself in the wider, social world and her ability to affect it. She learns how to:

- *Choose friends:* A child is born into her family, and the members of this family are immediately significant to her. But friends can be chosen, and a child thereby experiences her power to select the people she spends time with and cares about.
- *Comparatively assess her abilities:* Among peers, children learn to assess their abilities in relation to others. They learn that some children are quicker at learning how to read, some are more popular, some are stronger, some are more disruptive, and some are better at sports. A child may also learn that she finds math easier than others, or is particularly good at hockey or at making other children laugh.

- *Attract and entertain her peers:* The dynamics of peer relation-ships are so different from family dynamics that children come to know themselves in very different ways when they play with other children. They also acquire different skills—for example, they learn how to get other children's attention and keep them interested in a game or conversation.
- *Cooperate and share with others outside her family:* While the family is a ready-made unit, groups of friends have to be formed. A child learns how to play or work with peers, how to share her own ideas and plans.
- *Understand and empathize with others:* Other children become windows through which a child sees different emotional worlds. Children's conversations are filled with attempts to understand others' feelings. They experience their power to affect others as they comfort or quarrel with a friend.

Friendships are neither simple nor static. They give a child a sense of belonging, but they also present the risk of rejection. Coopera-tion breaks down, groups of close friends disband, problems arise between them. As psychologist Judy Dunn notes, "A child's sense of self efficacy is likely to come in large part from solving these problems, from having control over such social matters. In being effective in these matters, a core of children's feelings about them-selves is established." For a child to form a positive core of feelings about herself, she may need special coaching in the skills of mak-ing and maintaining friendships.

Making Friends

Some children are quite self-contained and need few friends. But, in general, children who feel themselves to be "outsiders" feel uncomfortable and are often unhappy. They long to be with others and feel inferior or deficient because they do not have friends.

"I'm so lonely in the playground, and it's like everyone's staring at me because I'm the only one who's alone," explained seven-year-old Alice.

"Everyone else is rushing around, shouting and playing and stuff. I just sort of watch them. It makes me sad—but I just stand around," said eight-year-old Mark.

Children who are isolated from others evaluate themselves in a more negative way than children who regularly play with others and have friends. An isolated child does not simply think she has a low social status; she also sees herself as having a range of problems: Socially isolated children describe themselves as worrying more, being more shy, having fewer friends, and being less attractive. They also tend to see themselves as less happy than other children.

Though we cannot stand beside a child on the playground, we can help her develop skills to negotiate difficult social situations. Just as we help her acquire the skill of riding a bike, we can teach her skills that are needed for joining games and making friends. After all, *the ability to solve problems, to negotiate difficulties, to overcome obstacles, to act with reasonable hope that one will succeed, are the defining points of self-esteem.* These abilities are also important in the social world of the child.

INITIATING A FRIENDSHIP

Some lonely or shy children lack experience or finesse in approaching and playing with other children. Some are simply too anxious and inhibited to approach another child. They may be frightened of being rejected, or they may simply not know how to approach—or accept overtures—from other children. They may be so tense that they seem "odd" or uninviting. These children can use our help in learning how to take steps toward establishing a friendship.

The process of making friends can be divided into:

- *greeting skills:* These involve a kind of friendly introduction, or displaying some version of "hello," whereby she invites another child to explore the possibility of friendship.
- *grounding the introduction:* This involves asking another child for information about himself and reciprocating by offering information about herself. Such preliminary steps may include inviting another child to join a game or requesting that she be included in a game.
- *rewarding an interaction:* A child can also learn how to reward others for interacting with her—by listening, laughing, appreciating another's input and elaborating on that input. She can learn to make another child feel good.

We can provide clear instructions and reminders to help our child use these skills.

INSTRUCTION: "Look, smile, say 'Hi,' to someone you might want to be your friend."

REMINDER: "She will probably return your greeting. If she doesn't, *she's* probably very shy. Either try again, or try someone else." The message is: "If the greeting doesn't work, you have lost nothing."

INSTRUCTION: "You could ask her name or where she lives, or whether she wants to play with you or simply stand next to you and chat. Tell her where you live, or what you like to do after school."

REMINDER: "Once you get this far, it's hard to lose. Another child will be pleased that you are interested in her." The message is: "You have already made a successful step. Keep going."

INSTRUCTION: "Don't forget to show her that you want to hear what she is saying. Try not to interrupt her, but keep the conversation going. We can practice conversations, if you like."

REMINDER: "There's no need to worry now. But she may still feel shy, and need to see that you still find her interesting." The message is: "You have done everything right. Now the challenge is to reassure her."

These instructions and reminders, with their implicit messages, are important for two reasons: First, they are effective; and second, just having them as rules of thumb will give a child confidence that she knows what do if she wants to make a friend. She is far more likely to initiate a friendship if she believes that her actions and responses can be effective.

MAINTAINING FRIENDS

For some lonely or shy children, the problem is not meeting new potential friends, but keeping the friendship going: A child may lack friends because she may be inexperienced and not know how to keep herself "in the game." She may be unable to handle the tensions and conflicts that arise, inevitably, in children's play. Such children may be able to handle the initial stages of making friends, but lack the skills to maintain friendships.

Often, parents make the mistake of supposing that if only their children are "nice," other children will like them. But friendship involves a range of interactions, and "being nice" is not always appropriate, and is seldom enough. In fact, friends also need to learn how to engage in conflict. Even when this conflict is framed as "play," it deals with important issues such as competition, comparisons, and challenge.

Franco, seven, explains that his tussles with Liam are so

enjoyable because "he always gets me down first, but I run faster." Liam explained that he knew he was growing when all he had to do to "flip Franco over is catch him in the knee." The boys, as friends, test their relative strength and fleetness. Each provides the other with a focus for competition and personal assessment.

Here are two girls involved in a game which demands more than "being nice" to keep it going:

"I have the hat," six-year-old Rhian informs her playmate as they root through a familiar dressing-up cupboard.

"No," Jill counters, "I wear the hat because I'm—you know—the silly lady."

"You're not silly. This isn't the silly lady game."

"It *is* . . . you said . . . anyway, I need it."

Each tugs momentarily on the hat. When Rhian lets go and Jill places it on her head, Rhian pushes it further down on Jill's head. Jill stumbles and falls back, hitting the floor with her bottom, but keeps hold of the hat on her head.

"I get it next," Rhian proclaims. "Because I'm the shopper—I work there—and I have to show it to you. I also get to press the buttons on the cash register and take your money."

"But I need it for a long time. You can wear the necklace."

These children's ability to negotiate the dispute keeps the game going and sustains the friendship. Friendship is not always easy rapport, but an interesting interaction that involves a series of problems and solutions: How to get the other child's attention; how to be fun to be with; how to cooperate and comfort and entertain. Children can learn these skills at a very early age. What prevents them, all too often, is adults' belief that they cannot manage on their own. Then children learn to be dependent on others to solve their interpersonal problems. Gripped by this dependency, a child may rush to an adult for help before drawing on her own problem-solving abilities. So quarrels between friends increase as a child fails to develop the skills to end such fights herself, and instead of learning how to resolve conflicts, she learns to manipulate adults either to comfort her or to intervene. These bad habits, however, can be reversed as we teach a child to think up many different ways of handling problems between people.

WAYS OF HELPING A CHILD RESOLVE DISPUTES WITH FRIENDS

Help her focus on her goal. Find out whether your child really wants to remain friends, or to play with a friend. It is important to know whether your child values the friendship or the play time with another child. Sometimes children quarrel with another child because they would rather be alone. If a child admits that she does want to sustain the friendship, or keep the play time going, then you can assume she is motivated to resolve the dispute.

You could say something like, "It is sometimes difficult to get on with people even though we like them. Your friend may be behaving badly, but even so, you've said you want to keep playing with her. So let's think about how to do this."

The message here is that relationships can give rise to problems, but if her goal is to form a friendship, these problems can be worked out.

Encourage a child to think up many different solutions to interpersonal problems. If a child sticks to one rule, and one rule only, then she will not know what to do when that rule does not work. Rhian could argue that she should keep the hat because she got it first: this is often a principle, or rule, used in child's play, a rule they learn from adults who try to negotiate fair play. If she sticks to that one rule and Jill refuses to accept it, however, the game is over and the friends are at odds. But she thinks of another solution: she can suggest a different game, and suggest a compromise whereby in this new game Jill has the hat—but only for a while.

If your child has some difficulty achieving this flexibility, then you might say something like, "It would be great to get your own way. That would be one way of ending the fight. But you said you wanted to stay friends with her. So you might not get just what you want at the moment. Do you want to play a different game, or change the one you're playing? Do you want to go out and do something different? Do you want to let your friend have her way for a while?"

This type of conversation coaches a child to think up different ways of resolving the conflict, and encourages her to envision a range of possible solutions.

Stimulate a child to anticipate consequences of her actions while she plays. Sometimes a child wants both to keep a friend and make a point. If Rhian insists upon "telling Jill off" or arguing about the fairness of her having the hat, the relations between the girls will deteriorate. This nearly happens, as they engage in a tug of war over the hat, but Rhian rapidly realizes what will happen if she sticks to this goal: the game will come to an unhappy end. So, Rhian decides to negotiate a solution: she will get the hat "next."

When a child has difficulty playing with friends, suggest she think about at least one thing she might have done to contribute to the falling out. You engage in some emotional coaching as you try to raise her awareness of how others are likely to respond to her behavior. You could say something like, "No one likes to be told off or shouted at, even when they're being unfair or difficult," or "Grabbing something is very likely to make someone want to grab back."

Here the message is not that your child is at *fault,* but that what she does may lead her friend to respond unpleasantly. If her behavior is not getting the results she wants, then she should change it.

Assure a child that she can make a positive difference to her role in games and her relationship with other children. Sometimes a child gives up on a friend, or a game, or simply gives in, because she does not believe she can actually have any positive effect on other children. When you help her consider the consequences of her actions, you alert her to the fact that a friend can be put off by certain behavior. It is also important to remind her that much of her behavior will have a positive effect. You might say, "I know you have lots of good ideas when you play at home. Could you share those ideas with your friends?" or "I bet your friend wants to know how much you want to play with her. Could you tell her? What do you think she'll say?"

Without issuing straightforward instructions, we can guide a child through conflicts or glitches with friends. Here are two examples, based on episodes in my parent/child workshops, which show how these measures work. In one workshop, Louise, seven, tries to join two other girls:

"No one's playing with me," she tells her mother.

"Why don't you ask whether you can play with them?" her mother suggests.

"They're playing together."

"You could play with them."

Louise eventually asks Sue and Anjana whether she can play with them. They say, "Yeah," and discuss her role in the game.

"You could be the person who gets the things—not the shopkeeper but the one who gets things into the shop," Sue suggests.

"The delivery person," Anjana agrees, but adds, "we'll only need you sometimes, because we already have stuff in the shop."

Louise talks to herself—first about the deliveries she was making to their shop, and then about her coat getting dirty, and then about how boring the game is because she does not have anything to do in it. She then wanders away.

"No one will play with me," she complains to me.

"Why not?" I asked.

"Because they have their own games and wouldn't let me play."

"Can you do something about it?" I asked.

"No. Because I don't have anyone to play with. I always ask. And I ask nicely. And they don't let me. They just don't let me and don't want to play with me."

Louise sees only one way of joining a game: She asks, "Can I play, too?" When asking does not get her what she wants, she gives up. Louise needs help establishing whether she really does want to play, and then she needs guidance to see how other children might respond (when she doesn't talk to them, but to herself); but most of all, she needs to be motivated by the belief that she can engage with the other children and make a difference to the game they play. Here is how the conversation eventually went:

"I heard them say you could join their game. And you want to?" I ask.

Louise nods.

"Why do you think they weren't playing with you?"

"I didn't have anything to do."

"Could you think of something to do?"

Louise shrugged, but after a pause said, "I could deliver the wrong thing."

"What might happen then."

"It would be silly," she laughed.

"It would be very silly—and fun. Why don't you try it?"

In another workshop, Sam, eight, was rejected by children because he "ruined their games." He would grab the rope that was used by the children for various games, both formal or informal. It was sometimes a skipping rope, and sometimes a snake used to frighten off others, and sometimes a rope used to tie other children up in games of cops and robbers. Sometimes it was a lead for a dog, or reins for an imaginary horse. Sam pushes his way into a group, and when he is pushed out, complains loudly to the supervisor that someone hit him.

Sam tries to join in the game by butting in, and hence disrupting it. As his strategies fail, he becomes more aggressive—he tries harder but uses the same ineffective strategy. He thinks the only thing he can do is behave more aggressively, and so his behavior deteriorates as he "tries harder." He is caught in the cycle of "trying to play" and then failing, and then blaming others. He becomes increasingly convinced that the problem "is not his fault," and increasingly convinced that he cannot solve the problem.

Sam needed to register the fact that his behavior was not having the effect he wanted—and he also needed some coaching to see that he could change his behavior. At the end of the lunch hour, I spoke to Sam, coaching him to use his own problem-solving abilities. The coaching messages are in italics:

ME: What happened? *(Identify the problem.)*

SAM: They wouldn't let me play. Joe hit me.

ME: Why did he hit you? *(Understand how the problem arose.)*

Sam shrugs: I wanted to play with the rope. He had a long turn with it.

ME: So what did you do? (*Understand your own role in the problem.*)

SAM (smiling): I hit him.

ME: How did Joe feel about that? (*Focus on others' feelings.*)

SAM: Angry. He hit me.

ME: How did you feel? (*Understand your own feelings.*)

SAM: Angry. I hit him.

ME: So both of you were angry, and neither of you got to play. What else could you have done? (*Think up a solution.*)

SAM: I could tell on Joe—that he wasn't letting me have a turn.

ME: What would happen then? (*Anticipate consequences.*)

SAM: You'd say, like, "Why can't you play nicely like the other children."

ME: That's not much help, is it? (*Assess possible consequences.*)

SAM: No, you ladies are no help.

ME: So what else could you do? (*Think up better solutions.*)

SAM: I could take it and say I'd give it straight back.

ME: Yes, you could try that. What would he do? (*Keep anticipating consequences and assessing them.*)

SAM: He'd say "Give it here!"

ME:: So what else could you do? (*Think up a better solution.*)

SAM: I could say it's a poison snake, and he'd better watch out.

ME: What might happen then? (*Anticipate consequences.*)

SAM (giggling): I don't know. Yech. He'd go—(and he shows how Joe might shake it at him.)

ME: That sounds like a good game. (*Put your best solution into practice.*)

SAM: Yeah!

Sam seems to know much more about people and their responses than is evident at first. He knows that his behavior makes other children angry, and that it will not get him what he wants. He knows that the grown-ups will refuse to intervene. Sam is able to enjoy the conversation in which I encourage him to envision different outcomes of different behavior. But this is not enough. For his behavior to change he needs to think of something else to do. When he is encouraged to do this, he becomes happy and excited. He quickly understands that this way of thinking might enable him to get what he wants and solve many of his problems.

Such conversations guide a child from the initial position:

The problem is out of my control.

Louise's starting point is that she has tried to play with the other girls, and the game did not take off; therefore, there is nothing she can do but complain to an adult.

Sam's starting point is that the other boys will not allow him to play, and that there is no way around that. The child gives up because he sees himself as having tried, but failed.

The conversations guide the child to a different perspective. Instead of doing nothing, or just complaining, Louise and Sam can make creative suggestions, which enhance the fantasy on which their games ride. Louise can introduce a mishap into the game, which will increase her involvement. Sam can come up with a creative way to join the game that relies on a cooperative fantasy and not aggression. The children have, themselves, come up with ideas of how to improve the quality of their play with friends. At the end of the coaching conversation the child's concluding position is:

I can do several things to join the game. And it will be fun to try my ideas out!

Choosing Friends and Retaining a Clear Sense of Identity

Friendship gives a child the opportunity to experience different aspects of her personality. Friends share experiences and interests, and also help define who she is. A child can choose friends, at least partly, on the basis of who she becomes in their company: Friends confirm and extend a child's identity.

"I want to be friends with Craig because he's not afraid of anything. He can climb anything. Like he just climbs, and when we're together we're both cool," Jim, age eight, explained to me.

"Bettina is as horse-mad as me. She lives on a *farm*. When I go there, see, there's this stables thing filled with tack. You can smell it and—I love the smell. When we're at school together—we just talk about her horses, and which one I'll ride when I next go there—and so I really like being with her," explained Liz, age ten.

For Jim and Liz, friendship blends envy and admiration. It involves borrowing another's strength and gaining access to another's possessions or skills.

This strategy of choosing friends who represent what a child wants to be, is called "active niche-picking." A child looks around and chooses her niche for herself. A child begins to choose an "identity environment" by making friends with other children who, she believes, are "like her" or whom she wants to be like. She has not chosen her parents or siblings or neighbors. Even her early friendships may have "happened" rather than been deliberately chosen. From the age of seven or eight, she plays an active part in choosing her friends and carving her niche in the social world.

Yet sometimes parents feel that a child's friend is not building up her identity but breaking it down. Friends do have an impact on a child's development, and sometimes this impact is negative. Here are some views of friends who seem to undermine rather than support a child's identity:

"I try to explain how important it is to work conscientiously, and he tells me that working is 'naff' or whatever the word of the day is. Because along with a different set of values, he learns a different language," Richard explained of his thirteen-year-old son Kevin.

Murray, age nine, became, his mother said, "a wild guy with his friends. He'll do anything to get their attention—once he even jumped off a bridge. There's really no judgment there, when he meets up with those boys, who just let him tag along because he's such a clown." For Murray, the excitement of other children's company, and the craving to join a group, made him risk anything.

Gil, also nine, longed for friends but was impeded from making them through a combination of shyness and aggression: "He'll say nothing for hours, and then will rush forward like a bull, trying to take his place in some game," his mother reported. "He's sensitive at home, with his little brother, but he can't play with children his own age. They tease him—talk about parties he's not invited to, make fun of the boots he wears—and it makes him miserable."

Sarah despaired over the influence peers were having on her eleven-year-old son Pete: "All I've done to build up his confidence after the divorce is being knocked down again by these guys who are bullying him."

Kevin was building up a false, misguided sense of strength through his peers, and was learning to devalue his family's values. Murray worked so hard to please his friends that he put his physical well-being at risk. Gil was made miserable by his inability to connect positively with his peers. Pete was learning, through his experience of being bullied, that he was weak and worthless. Each child's parent voices concern alongside a sense of helplessness as their child is sucked into the world of peers, away from the values, the encouragements, and even the language of the family.

But parents are never helpless. We can always reach our children—with the right techniques and the right strategies. First, we should understand why a child can lose her values and judgment among friends. Then I'll offer guidelines for giving our child the power to remain herself while she interacts with friends.

WHY A CHILD RELINQUISHES HER IDENTITY TO A FRIEND

The most common reasons that children bury the better aspects of themselves in a friendship are the desire for self-definition (a sense of identity) and the need to belong to a group.

Sometimes, to one child, other children appear absolutely certain about who they are. Another child's personality will seem brilliantly well-defined, while her own seems rough-edged or blurred. She may then decide: "I don't know who I am, but I know who she is, and if I become like her, then I'll know who I am."

If a child engages in this *identity-borrowing process,* she takes a short cut in her own identity development. She looks around and says, "I will be her," rather than discover who she is. A parent's goal is to reinforce a child's own sense of identity.

Gail was confused by her daughter Rachel's "chameleon" character: "I'd think she was a natural mimic if I didn't know she was utterly serious. Now she has a twelve-year-old friend—a year older than her—who wants to be a model, and there she is, wanting to be a model, too, and starting to dress and walk just like this other girl. But a few months back she was tuned into Jasmin. I swear, she began to look Indian. She talked like her and moved like her, and wanted me to cook all the things Jasmin ate."

With children like Gail, a parent's goal is to ground the child in her own identity. Here are ways this can be done:

1. *Remind her that her thoughts and opinions are of special interest to you.* Make a deliberate effort to ask her opinion about a person in the news or the color of a carpet or the taste of an apple. Show interest in her answers, and show that you remember them. She will get the message that her everyday experience is significant.

2. *Refrain from endorsing the importance of her friends.* Sometimes, inadvertently, parents tease a child about a friend who, they know, is always on her mind. Never ask about the dominating friend. At the same time, do not reject information your child gives you about the friend—this, too, may reinforce the friend's significance. Listen to your child talk about her friend without any special emotion, and then go on to other topics. In this way, you diffuse the focus on the friend.

3. *Encourage her to develop, or retain, her own interests.* Your child will have abilities and interests that the friend does not have. Make sure your child continues to develop these. They may be interests or enthusiasms that you do not particularly value— such as interest in a soap opera or pop group. Nonetheless, this may be a time to encourage her as she marks out her own territory.

4. *Take extra care to respect her "territory" in the home.* Children always need their own space, respect for their belongings, and someone to listen to them when they talk. When a child seems "submerged" by a friend, make sure these needs are met as fully

as possible. By showing respect for her individual needs, you can assure her that she has a strong identity.

PEER PRESSURE

A child's willingness to change herself and her values to mesh with those of her friends can come from a desire to fit in or belong or be accepted. This process is commonly known as peer pressure. Peer pressure is often a form of bullying, whereby the child is made to feel inadequate unless she "proves" herself by doing what others do. This inadequacy can focus on small things, such as hairstyle and clothes, or on much larger issues, such as drugs and sex and high-risk behavior (involving cars, late nights, vandalism, dangerous stunts). Yet a child may accept these dangers for the comfort of belonging to a group.

When Greg, thirteen, formed a friendship with Steve, his status at school was raised: Now he was in with a group of boys that other people took notice of. But to keep "in" with them, he had to stay out late, have money for bus fares and fast food and, above all, never be seen to be accountable to his parents. The rules of discipline, which had carefully been established over the years, were now challenged constantly.

Greg wants to borrow "status" from his friends. He feels stronger and more adventurous when he is with them, and he likes sharing their popularity.

The goal of Greg's parents is to stick by *their* rules. This can be achieved "simply" but may require great effort. In such situations, parents could follow these guidelines:

1. *Parents must be consistent.* Nothing has changed in their home, and nothing has shifted their values, just because Greg wants his lifestyle to change.

2. *Parents must be firm.* The normal leeway that can be allowed a child who is not deliberately testing every rule and family policy cannot be given to a child who wants to follow some other, unacceptable set of rules.

3. *Parents should be prepared to be disliked for a while.* With his "high status" friends on his side, Greg may become more critical of his parents, but if they sit tight, remain consistent and firm, he will ease off.

4. *We should welcome a child back, when he is his "old self."* A child who feels the influence of friends may seem "completely different"—but usually this difference is temporary. When he returns to being a pleasant and confiding child, accept him naturally, without taking revenge, without teasing him, indeed, without comment.

HELPING A CHILD RESIST PEER PRESSURE

A child who does not conform may be threatened with exclusion. The most common way a child experiences exclusion is through teasing. Children can be immensely cruel and well organized in their teasing. Whereas boys tend to prove their power with physical aggression, girls are often more subtle, making apparently casual or "helpful" comments about another girl's appearance or her reputation. "That sweater is an interesting color, but it doesn't go with your hair" or "I think you should know, just for your own good, that always sitting next to Jim on the schoolbus doesn't look right."

When a child faces this abuse, a parent's goal is to teach her how to assert herself. This may be difficult, especially if belonging to the group is her prime goal. Nonetheless, we can remind her how to assert her confidence and maintain self-esteem in friendship. The most effective way is to propose certain questions she can put to herself. In this way, we avoid "giving lectures," but we nonetheless encourage our child to reassess the friendship:

1. *Can she express her own opinions, even when they differ from her friends?* A parent can remind a child that however much she thinks she has in common with her friends, she will—and should—think differently about some things. You can use the individuality that she already has to remind her of this: "I know you think this friendship is good for you. But just think about whether you are comfortable being different from them. Think about what it means if you are not."

2. *Is she as important as her friend?* Remind her that friendship is a two-way processes. In a real friendship each person is equally important. Is she able to ask for help, as well as to offer it? Is she able to borrow clothes from her friend, as well as lend them? Can she change the time of a meeting or suggest an "agenda" for an outing? Suggest she count the number of times she says to her friend, "I don't mind" or "It's up to you."

3. *Can she complain effectively?* All friendships have their ups and downs. If a friend offends a child, she should be able to discuss this. "I was upset when you told Joe what I told you" or "I felt sad when you asked Amy instead of me to go to the nurse with you" are reasonable complaints that a child should be able to voice in a friendship. Suggest she try voicing her complaints and see what happens.

4. *Can she refuse unreasonable requests?* If a child cannot say to a friend, "I'm not happy doing that" or "I'm not allowed to do that" or "I don't want to lend you that blouse" or "I don't have time to go with you," then the friendship is governed by a bully's rules—and therefore it is not a true friendship between equals.

These questions provide her with the tools for assessing the friendship herself. They also give her the message: "You are valuable and should be treated well by your friends." This confidence is essential in making *good* friends.

OFFERING SUPPORT THROUGH THE UPS AND DOWNS OF FRIENDSHIP

Parents are sometimes stunned by the punishment a child is willing to take in order to keep a friend. Naomi and Duncan, both aged eight, regularly fought, but just as regularly played together. Yet day after day, Naomi complained to her mother that Duncan "bossed her around," was "mean to her," or even "kept punching her." But she wanted to keep him as a friend, "because I like walking to school with him."

Molly Ann and Ruth, both aged seven, were neighbors and hence convenient playmates, but Ruth felt that Molly Ann always "made fun of her" (by mimicking her or criticizing her family) and "put [her] down" (by boasting). But she refused to heed her mother's advice not to play with her, because "outside school she's nice."

Charles, thirteen, put up with Nick's ridicule of his height and his hair, explaining that Nick was "not mean all the time, and sometimes all right."

The goal parents have in such situations is to help a child track the pain within the friendship so that the child can decide whether to mend or end the friendship.

Help her register her pain. When a child comes to us with complaints about a friend, or descriptions of being excluded from a game or a party, acknowledge the real pain she feels.

Instead of saying: "Don't pay any attention to them" or "They're only teasing," say: "That must be upsetting" or "Your feelings must be hurt" or "You sound both angry and sad."

Injunctions to ignore her friends, or minimize the pain a friend's behavior causes, are ways of invalidating her distress. She will feel more alone, because the message is, "You have no reason to feel bad." She will feel less alone if her feelings are understood.

Help her define her goals. Does she want to continue with the friendship, even though it causes her pain? If not, then the matter is closed: the friendship should end. If she wants to keep the friendship, then she must change it so as not to be constantly hurt.

Work through the procedure of resolving disputes with friends. This means you may be going over old material, but that does not matter. Your child may need reminding and help as she:

- *identifies the problem:* Before a child tries to mend a friendship, it is helpful for her to identify what bothers her. Is her friend teasing her too much? Is a certain kind of teasing intolerable—such as teasing about a boyfriend or her appearance—or is it the way a friend treats her in group? Is she upset by something specific that the friend did—such as discuss her personal problems with someone else? It is far more effective to go to work on a specific problem, than on some ill-defined dissatisfaction, such as "She's been bugging me lately."

- *thinks up different ways of resolving disputes:* In some cases we can encourage her to think of ways this can be done: "Could you talk to your friend about the teasing, and ask her why she does it, and whether she knows it hurts you?" The feelings of both friends should be acknowledged and considered.

- *thinks about—and notes—the results of her actions:* Does she provoke her friend? Can she find a way to avoid her friend's teasing or irritation? Can she change her behavior to get a better response?

- *assesses her strategies:* If she finds ways of resolving disputes, then she will gain confidence. If nothing she does has a positive effect, then she will have to come up with new problem-solving methods or end the friendship.

As we remind our child of the standards of real friendship, we also remind the child that she is worth too much to accept poor treatment from anyone. Her ability to assess friendships both expresses and supports her confidence.

Preventing Prejudice from Harming Our Children's Self-Esteem

In this chapter we have been looking at the ways in which children learn and develop through friendships. As they play with other children, console them, and entertain them, they gain awareness of their own social power. They learn that they can interact with others, solve problems that arise with other people, and have a positive impact on relationships.

If a child has difficulty achieving this important pathway to self-esteem—if some shyness or lack of confidence or awkwardness blocks the ability to make friends and play with others—then parents can give special encouragement. Some children need extra help developing those social skills of greeting others, engaging their attention, and sharing responses with them. Other children need extra help keeping the friendship going. If we guide a child to think about many possible solutions to interpersonal conflicts, we give her skills to solve the inevitable problems that arise within friendships, as well as the problems that will arise in her future dealings with people.

However, some children are excluded not because they lack the skills to make and keep friends, but because others hold prejudices against the race or religion or culture to which they belong. Even as more and more people are becoming sensitive to the realities of a multicultural society, minority children continue to suffer repeated incidents of discrimination at school—in the form of verbal or physical assaults, racist comments, and implicit messages that exclude minority children from participating in certain activities, or using space available to others.

In a recent study, three-quarters of minority children had experienced some racial abuse recently, and more than a third of minority children experienced repeated incidents of discrimination. When children suffer from other people's prejudices, parents must help prevent these prejudices from harming their children's self-esteem. The ways that many prejudices are structured into our society's laws, language, and customs are subtle and varied. The ways children pick up on these prejudices and respond to them are only sketched here. The problems of prejudice—both for those who harbor it and for those who receive it—would fill a series of books written by experts. Here are some starting points.

PARENTS MUST TRY TO PREVENT A CHILD FROM INTERNALIZING THE PREJUDICES OF OTHERS.

All children pick up messages about good and bad, beautiful and ugly, normal and odd, from the books they read, the television and films they watch, the toys they play with, the language they learn. Often these books, programs, films, and ways of speaking carry the assumption that one race, religion, nationality, or sex is better than others.

When, for example, an African-American, Hispanic, or Asian child learns to read from books that portray the normal child as white, when she learns to admire dolls that have blue eyes and smooth blond hair, then she may come to think that her own features, or her family's way of speaking or acting, are less important, less valuable than features and behavior represented as typical of those belonging to the majority culture. If, further, she learns that others label her "nigger," "Paki," "slit eyes," or "spic," she may discover that hatred of her (as a member of a minority race, religion, or culture) is built into the culture in which she lives and whose language she speaks, or is learning to speak.

She may eventually *internalize* prejudices against her: She may come to believe that she cannot be beautiful because she does not have the features considered beautiful by the dominant culture. She may pick up on a teacher's doubt that she is smart or reliable, and so come to doubt herself. She may come to believe that she deserves others' contempt or distrust.

This is a terrifying effect of prejudice. With low self-esteem and meager expectations, a child's motivation is undermined: Why should she try, when no one will give her a chance? Or, she may believe that she cannot succeed, because others must have "some reason" for the way they treat her. In such situations, parents must work extra hard to instill confidence in a child.

The skills a child needs to withstand prejudice are not different in kind from those every child needs, but they need to have a stronger handle. They need to be ready-to-use day and night. As Jenny, a parent of Gary, seven, and Andrew, nine, explained:

These children are not just like a white kid who's bullied. Because the white kid who's bullied leaves that situation and goes home to watch television where he has no trouble identifying with the best kids there, and he walks in the best neighborhood without anyone thinking there's something wrong because he's there, and he doesn't have to see—one hundred times a day, some days—that sweating look in the white man's eye because he isn't white.

Jenny points out that the young white boy who is bullied can move into a more comfortable context: When he watches films he can identify with the "good" boy; when he reads a comic book, he is the same race as the hero; when he walks into a store to buy chewing gum, his skin color will not give rise to suspicion. Jenny sees that her children—and African-American children in general—have to deal daily with many different contexts in which they are, implicitly or explicitly, bullied. Other parents share this sense that the greatest harm of discrimination comes from the multiple messages of prejudice, as Roberta explains:

My children will hear at least five parallel scripts when they make their way into the world. It may be different things my daughters hear and my boy. But my oldest—my son—who's now fifteen, already talks about that creepy feeling of being typecast. Someone will give you a chance, but one foot wrong and they slip you into a mold. It's a real tight fit. You want your kids to have a strong sense of who they are, and where they're going, and what the odds against them are. You want to pass on this strength to them. You want to pack them full of the Lord's love and your love.

Her husband, Garth, concurred: "If only they know how much they're worth—like the Lord knows and we know—then they won't be beaten down, and they won't go stupid with shame, and they'll walk tall and proud."

All of us, as parents, can help children withstand prejudice. Here are some guidelines:

Forewarn a child of the prejudice she is likely to experience. The best message is: "Don't expect prejudice, but don't be surprised when you see it. Show that you are trying to bypass prejudice by looking at people when you speak to them and being yourself. When they're uncomfortable with that, and when they seem to stay uncomfortable, then take care of whatever business you may have with them (check out the library book, ask the question) and then terminate the conversation."

Your goal is to prepare her for others' prejudices, without creating unnecessary suspicion of other people.

Offer a historical account of this prejudice. To understand is not to forgive, but if a child understands how extensive and long-term certain prejudice is, then she is far less likely to take it personally. She will come to understand that prejudice sometimes is a way of avoiding the great sense of guilt a member of the dominant culture may have toward a minority. Moreover, if she knows the history of her race or religion, she is less likely to feel rejected by prejudice, and more likely to see that the fault lies with the people who are prejudiced.

Explain the forms prejudice may take—on the street, at school, among friends. Some common ways of expressing prejudice are:

- name-calling
- low expectations of what she can do
- unjustified fear (that she will show violence, or that she is "dirty" or has some disease)

- exclusion from parties or outings
- extreme uneasiness in her presence
- failure to "see" her, or to take her presence into account, or to meet her eye

But far more insidious are forms of prejudice that crop up in books and paintings and language. She may find that no member of her race appears in such cultural products—or, if someone does, the representation is stereotypical—devoid of individuality. It will be helpful if she can identify such "blindness" to her people in history, mainstream literature, or films. This is a challenging learning process, for parents and children alike.

Give a child some sense of what her options are when confronted with prejudice. There are many positive ways to deal with prejudice:

- A child can "walk away" from it, and refuse to engage with a person who reveals prejudice.
- She can engage with the person who feels prejudice and try to change her views.
- She can ignore it, act as though it isn't there.
- She can bring it into the open and suggest that the problem be discussed.

It is important to pass on to her what you have learned about handling prejudice, and then ask for feedback from your child so that she can find the strategy that is most effective for her. These discussions will help her be an active observer of discrimination—and this critical eye will support her confidence.

Assure her that she can model herself and her future on anyone she chooses. Just as important as celebrating one's own race, and finding members of one's own race to admire and emulate, is the ability to make use of a multiracial culture—to make use of every potential.

Racism is a form of bullying, of targeting a child for being "different" and banding together with others in order to exclude and terrorize a child. In defense, a child may try to deny or disguise her difference in order to fit in. This can lead to loss of self-esteem in the following ways:

- By trying to fit in, and adopt the behavior, language, or attitudes of the majority culture, a child may feel that she herself is worthless, and can only be of worth when she is like others. She sees acceptance in terms of not being herself.

- By devaluing the culture of her family and community, she may be breaking links to those people who can provide emotional support.

- By trying to change herself as she changes from one world to another, she becomes confused, and feels out of place in both worlds.

Alternatively, a child may stick so close to friends of her own race that she refuses to take advantage of other opportunities. Here are the stories of some children's conflict between their wish to achieve, and their wish to belong:

Eduardo began eight grade as a strong student. "He was hard working, with a good head on his shoulders," his father reported. "Always he showed good judgment. He was a boy you could rely on, a boy everyone trusted. Now something's got into him. He had this chance to be in a good stream. He was heading for it. Now, all of a sudden, he gets lazy. Now—now when it really matters, he won't put in that effort."

Was the work getting harder? I asked Eduardo. Was school less interesting than it had been six months ago? Was he in love?

Was he on drugs? The problem was none of these things; his story made tragic sense.

"All my life my father tells me that if I work hard I can get ahead, go to college, do well in life. But now it doesn't seem so easy. Even at school I can see what it's like outside my group of friends. Before junior high, it was very comfortable, very cosy. But now it would be more difficult to leave my friends. And those friends are not going to be streamed. What good would it do me anyway? Those [white] kids think of us as scum. Every class of theirs I'd walk into, I'd have to show my papers. There's hard work and more hard work, and no one to help you. It's not that I'm doing anything on purpose, but I feel new weights on me, and I can't focus like I used to."

Eduardo's father has tried to sustain his son's motivation, insisting that good goals can be met, and that honest effort is worthwhile. But for Eduardo, the new school has shown him that the world outside is unfriendly, even dangerous. He needs his friends— other Mexican American children—for support and safety. He feels that hostility towards American Mexicans is increasing: "showing his papers" refers to the new California ruling against allowing children of illegal immigrants into public schools; but it also registers the common prejudice that Hispanic children do not belong in the upper streams: Each day, he believes, he would have to prove his worth.

Other psychologists reported similar reluctance among minority students to leave their peers behind. One boy told educational psychologist Patricia Phelan, "I wouldn't let them put me in a higher track because I wanted to be with my friends." Another said, "Being Mexican means being popular, cutting classes, acting crazy." For these boys, the need to preserve one world prevented them from making a successful sojourn in another. It is the same conflict we have learned to expect in girls, who have been shown, in some studies, to be concerned that academic achievement will leave them bereft of friends. When students try to change or mold themselves in order not to be "weird" and to "fit in," they may devalue aspects of their home and community cultures.

A Mexican American girl, fourteen, who was in a higher track than the majority of Hispanic students in her school, said that other students "probably think of me as weird, because they probably have this view that most Hispanics are dumb . . . Maybe by the end of the year they will realize that I belong." A Vietnamese American girl, a freshman in Patricia Phelan's study, said she "got nervous over little things" because she felt alone—because there were more of "them." As these children entered classes in which they felt closer to white, middle-class culture, they worried, "Am I going to make friends?" "What will people think of me?" "Am I really smart?" "Can I really do the work?" "Will I sound dumb?" And alongside their concern at being outsiders, they worried about being disloyal to their own family and upbringing: "I don't ever want to feel less black than I do today," insisted thirteen-year-old Lucy. "And it's hard making friends, while all the time I want to say how different I am."

Eduardo sees joining a higher stream as dangerous: He will lose the support of his friends. The Vietnamese American girl Li is afraid that she will be disloyal if she succeeds in her school. Their parents could coach them into greater confidence:

1. *Achievement is never disloyal.* Eduardo may leave his friends if he goes into a "streamed" class, but he is betraying no one. By being different, he is constructing new visions and possibilities

for everyone. Li's parents could tell her they are proud of her achievement. Cultural transitions are highly complex, but a parent's acceptance of some change and integration goes a long way with a child.

2. *Never believe other people's negative views.* Eduardo has difficulty showing each teacher his credentials. It is discouraging to have to keep proving himself, but Eduardo's father could remind him, "I said you could do it—not that it would be easy. Other people will doubt you, but each time you prove yourself, you have reason to know that you can do it again." The message is that the recurrence of these challenges should increase his confidence.

3. *Minority status is never an excuse to fail.* There are many reasons why achievement takes more effort and requires more support for a minority child. Parents can acknowledge this: "I know it's hard, and I know it's harder for you than it should be," we might say. But all children have to try, learn, and care—about themselves and others. Eduardo's father could say, "If you give up on yourself, then prejudice has won a great battle. You may fail, because anyone can fail, but that is not a reason to stop trying."

   As a child's difficulties are acknowledged, and as a parent offers support for her continued efforts, the message is: "If it's harder for you, it's that much more a triumph when you don't give up."

4. *Overcoming prejudice is a personal triumph.* Eduardo's father can register his son's frustration at others' prejudice, while reminding him that he is achieving something important when he resists it.

If a parent coaches a child in these ways, he offers a *structured pep talk* whose purpose is not simply to comfort or cheer a child up. This type of conversation frames the difficult experience of prejudice in positive ways. With this coaching, prejudice can be identified as a problem that demeans others—never the child at whom it is directed—and sets her a challenge she can continue to meet through her life.

Friends for Life

Some of this chapter deals with the problems children have with friends, and the threat peers' influence can have on our child, with how a child's wish to belong to a group or stay loyal to her friends may actually reduce her confidence for life. But the primary message of children's friendships is positive. A child's close friendships are essential to emotional growth. As parents, we can engage in emotional coaching to help a child understand the human world, but we cannot teach her everything. With "best friends" or "chums," a child discovers new perspectives about people like her—and she discovers, too, how different people can be from her. She learns how to make herself understood, for as she talks with her friends, she practices ways of expressing her ideas and feelings. She also experiences and develops her capacities to listen to others and to comfort, encourage, and organize others. Personal interaction leads to skills that will be necessary to her future relationships—not only close personal relationships, but also those with fellow students and colleagues or clients or bosses or people she simply passes in the street. We should not neglect coaching her in the skills needed to maintain confidence with friends.

nine

Adolescence: New Touchpoints for Self-Esteem

Many parents feel they lose that crucial intuition about what a child needs and feels when a child passes into the realm of adolescence. For some parents, adolescence seems to transform their lovable, responsive child into a stranger— sometimes into a monster bent on making life hell. We may feel at our wit's end in dealing with teenagers, who express more indifference than love, and who develop an iron-cast resistance to parental advice.

"A shutter goes down when I try to talk to her," John remarked of his fourteen-year-old daughter. "There's this blankness. Like she putting up a sign 'Not at home.' " Fifteen-year-old Steve's mother said that "When I ask him how his day was, he looks at me like I'm some weirdo, some alien whose language he can't understand. Sometimes he'll even repeat it to himself—muttering, you know, 'How was your day,' as though he's really trying to make sense of it—or maybe marvelling over the nonsense of it."

Other parents describe similar techniques a teenager uses to keep her distance. There was fifteen-year-old Jessica's "teenage eye-roll," as she looked to the sky for guidance as to how to deal with her difficult parents. There was fourteen-year-old Emmanuel's "porcupine coat," which, his mother said, he now wore whenever she tried to hug him: "He used to be such a great cuddler. Now he raises those spines when I come near him, and I have a choice to stay away or get spiked." There was Hamish's "adolescent lip thrust" as his lower lip jutted out in reply to a parent's suggestion. "Mo-other" with the elongated vowel exhaled in a sigh, and the high-pitched protest "Mom!" or "Dad!" are frequently heard from teenage children.

Adolescence is a phase during which a child leaps towards adulthood. It can also be a dangerous phase, during which a child may become distracted and distraught. How can we help our teenager sustain her self-esteem and respectful regard of her future self, when she seems determined not to listen to us? How do we stop ourselves from becoming nags, as our great concern for her well-being makes us speak, even as her eyes warn us that she won't listen.

"I hear a voice I never thought I'd hear in myself. 'Get down to work. Stop frittering away your time. Can't you make friends with *nice* kids?' This is the voice of my father—but I'm the one talking. So when Raine throws her eyes to the ceiling—'There he goes again' she's thinking—I know she's right, but it's the only thing I know how to do."

Many parents also feel that whatever they say has a negative effect: "I tell Greg it's time to do his homework, and all of a sudden I get 'I was going to, but now I don't want to.' Or he says, 'If you just stop nagging me, I might get around to doing it.' So I'd do better, I guess, to keep my mouth shut. But how can you, when you worry so much about his future?"

Special Threats to Self-esteem in Adolescence

Teenagers continue to need their parents, even though they may seem to reject us. In fact, they need our support and recognition more than ever as they confront new sources of self-consciousness and self-doubt, which can put self-esteem at risk. As they become aware of just how much is expected of them—in terms of independence, appearance (their "looks"), performance in school, status among friends—they often feel unworthy, unequal to the task. They may hide behind facades—playing either the silly, devil-may-care role, or the tough, can-handle-anything-myself role. As a child puts a false self on display, she worries constantly about being "found out," exposed, or shown up to be "a fake."

Since teenagers are better than younger children at hiding their self-doubts, we may have to be on a special lookout for a teenager's loss of self-esteem.

Does your teenager suddenly give up many of the things that interested her and inspired her as a child? Some children suddenly lose both confidence and enthusiasm as adolescence strikes. We should try to find out why an eager child suddenly becomes a sullen teenager, or why what was once a delight is now a "bore." Our goal is then to make sure there are no unnecessary impediments to her pursuing her interests.

To reach this goal we can follow many of the suggestions made earlier for alleviating depression in a child. The ennui that settles on a teenager is a form of depression. We therefore have to clear away the "I can't/don't want to do anything" mood. A parent can encourage a lethargic teenager to explain why she is dropping activities or plans. When our fourteen-year-old gives up the swimming, gymanstics, or acting to which she was once so committed, we can help her understand her own reasons and help redirect her. Instead of asking questions that imply criticism ("What's wrong with you? Why don't you go to the gym anymore?") express empathy with her feelings ("You seem discouraged") and ask genuinely information-seeking questions ("Is there a problem at the gym?"). If we help her identify the problem (Does she think she is too fat to do gymnastics? Does she think she is insufficiently muscular to work out among her friends? Is she being teased? Or have her interests genuinely changed?) then we can help banish the impediment to the activity, or find an alternative one.

We can also lift her from the doldrums by suggesting she describe her ideal future. What, we can ask, would she like to be doing ten years from now? If she engages positively in this exercise, we can then think of ways her future goals (being in an interesting job, travelling, designing clothes or engines) can be linked up with something she could do today, this week, or this month.

Does she spend a great deal of time thinking about her appearance, either in a positive or negative way? Young people are under enormous pressure to "look the part," to gain the attention and approval of their peers. They face daily reminders of what they should look like and how they should dress and what shape their bodies should be. Their peers note and criticize their appearance, and this concern for how they look is rigorously enforced by films, television, magazines, and advertisements, wherein they see "models" of what they "should" be. Uncertain themselves of who they are, they can all too easily find "proof" all around them that they are not what they should be.

Some teenagers, in the confusion they feel when they undergo physical changes, want to hide their bodies; some want to display, but also disguise their bodies. In either case, the adolescent is plagued by self-consciousness, which drains her energy in other fields. Feeling awkward, she may also feel unlovable. Sarah, fifteen, said she could not imagine why her father would want her—overweight and spotty—when he had his perfect new baby girl to adore. Adolescents may seem to push a parent away because they find it difficult to believe that a parent still loves them.

Some young people try to disguise or manipulate their maturing bodies by starving themselves. The aim of compulsively dieting teenagers is often to erase all signs of sexual maturity, to hold on to the simplicity of a child's physique. Such children urgently require professional help, for eating disorders endanger their health; but they also need, as does every teenager, special reassurance about a parent's ongoing love for her as she matures physically.

TO HELP A CHILD WITHSTAND HER SELF-CONSCIOUSNESS AND UNCERTAINTY, WE CAN:

1. *Show her the admiration we still feel for her as our "wonderful, special child."* We can express admiration for her face, her figure, and her hair. Simple, noncomparative admiration is most effective. "Your hair is such a lovely color," or "You have a charming smile." Don't be discouraged if a teenager appears to be indifferent to such praise: She still hears it and gains confidence from it.

2. *Give her more physical space than she had as a child, without cutting off all physical contact.* We must take cues from a child as to how much physical affection she welcomes, but we can cer-

tainly show her some—in the form of hugs (though she may resist kisses), in the form of friendly pats (though she may now hate the squeezes and tickles she loved as a child).

3. *As we teach her whatever new lessons she needs for grooming a teenage body, we must remember that her body is not ours, and she does have the right to decorate it and style it to her liking.* Fighting over clothes and hairstyles is not worth the battle (though tattooing and body piercing may well be!).

4. *Do your level best not to criticise her appearance.* Teenagers are so touchy about their appearance that they pick up on the slightest criticism. And we must beware of barbed compliments, such as, "I like your hair like that. It doesn't look so greasy" or "Those trousers are nice. They make your hips look thinner." Remember, teenagers are loaded down with self-consciousness. We should not add to it.

5. *Protect her from sexual harassment.* Teasing about one's appearance, or experiencing any kind of sexual harassment can cause a terrible blow to a teenager's confidence. When this confidence is struck a severe blow, a young person may withdraw, and give up activities or friends or goals she once valued highly. Remind her that her body is never a suitable target for mockery or lewdness, and any comments about it from her classmates, from passers-by, from other parents, should be treated as seriously as racial or ethnic discrimination. If you help her identify this kind of attention as a form of bullying, she will be better equipped to confront and resist it.

6. *Tolerate her mood swings.* A teenager undergoes frequent mood changes. Sometimes life looks good, and sometimes everything seems miserable. Her behavior may vacillate, too: one moment she may seem more mature than you, and the next she will be more infuriatingly childish than her nine-year-old brother. But if you give her a hard time about these natural fluctuations in

mood and maturity, she may be even more confused by them herself.

So be ready to smile, even when your child looks glum. There is no need to take offense at her sour look and curled lip (though you may well want to put a stop to any verbal abuse, such as name-calling or swearing or shouting). Even when she is like a porcupine with raised quills, you can offer affection in the form of hug, pats, and terms of endearment: When a child does not return signs of affection, she is still likely to be glad to receive them.

Sustaining Motivation in the Teenage Years

Sometimes an eager and adventurous child may turn into an adolescent who seems to have no sense of direction. Adolescence is often a time during which young people become aware of how complex and difficult adult life is. This may take the wind out of their sails. What seemed easy may now seem difficult. What was worth working toward may now seem out of reach.

Many teenagers feel discouraged as they face the hurdles of tests and school entrance requirements. They may put forth an appearance of not caring, but the great majority of teenagers are in fact very anxious about school grades and worry about meeting a parent's expectations.

"I keep the best front I can, talking upbeat about school and stuff. But there's going to be that day that comes around when I have to show them my school report, and it just isn't going to be good enough—not like my sister's was, not like they expect. Sometimes I think it's because I can't concentrate, and sometimes it just seems too much . . . like I'm not really that good. But I keep try-ing, and keep smiling like I think I'm doing it, even though I know I'm gradually sinking." For Jeremy, fifteen, his inability to meet his parents' expectations was a source of shame, which he disguised with "upbeat talk about school," staving off the day of exposure by an inadequate report card.

Maria, fifteen, was anxious about leaving her friends behind as she performed academically better than they, and then dealing with the isolation of being one of the few Hispanics who, in her school, were in the top stream. "My mom thinks I'm a natural ge-nius. You know, straight A's without the kind of effort I secretly know it takes. 'You'll be fine. You study hard, you'll be fine,' she tells me when I go off to sit the S.A.T.s. But there are things other peo-ple know, just know without trying, and there are these huge gaps I have—maybe learning English a little late . . . You know how there are some things that are so difficult to catch up on? It isn't only Mom. I can't let the other kids see how hard it is. The kids in my class would think, 'I always knew she didn't belong,' and my friends—well, they'd say, 'Why sweat it?' Well, I sweat it for my mom. I know what she wants for me."

Repeatedly teenagers cite parents' pressure on them to do well in school as the most common form of family stress. Children who are at most risk of failing to live up to a parent's expectation feel this stress the most—though they are perceived as feeling it the least. They are at risk of being caught in a web of disappointment. Stuck to a sense of failure, paths ahead are blocked—both in real-ity, because they need to succeed to move forward, and in their own minds, because they do not expect, and no longer try, to succeed. For most teenagers, concern with academic achievement, with good grades and good results on standardized tests, with the re-alization of long-term education goals, create pressures that are sometimes difficult to withstand. In one study of two city high schools in California, it was found that 85% of the students planned to go on to a four-year college after graduation, and 95% of the students said that they worried about grades, that they were anxious about meeting expectations set by their parents, that they sometimes despaired of achieving their own goals or getting into a good college. They also worried about athletic achievement and social acceptance and attachments.

TO HELP OUR TEENAGER TOLERATE THESE PRESSURES AND SUSTAIN HER GOALS, WE CAN:

1. *Help her organize her time.* Teenagers frequently become overloaded with commitments to friends, to social events, to sports. It takes skill to set priorities. We can help teenagers develop this skill by discussing their aims, what they have to do to fulfill those aims, and what they may have to give up.

   You might suggest that she make a list of things she wants to do this semester, or this year. Then the list could be prioritized—the activities or goals she values most would come first. If the list of activities or goals is simply too long, then suggest she decide what to keep in, and what to leave out. If she is not sure whether the list is realistic, suggest that she draw up some kind of schedule to show when she might do what she hopes to do. She may then see that she is being unrealistic, without being simply told by you.

   Encourage her then to track her success in organizing her time. If she sticks to the most important activities on her list, is she now feeling less pressure? Is she able to meet more of her goals? If not, then may the list be reassessed? If she feels "on top of things," then she might want to add something to the list.

   In this way, you help her gain control over her time without simply "ordering her around." She can gain confidence not only by doing what she does well, but also by having some control over what she does and when.

2. *Acknowledge her self-doubts.* We may be inclined to cheer a child up by saying "You'll be fine," but she may hear this as "I don't want to listen to your problems." If a child is anxious about her schoolwork or an exam, suggest ways she can ease the anxiety: take practice exams, get help with the homework, let the teacher know she is worried. Read her doubts not as self-defeating gloom, but as a problem that you will help her work on.

3. *Align your expectations with a child's abilities.* Jeremy felt that he was disappointing his parents by not doing as well as his sister. Maria felt her parents thought she could easily compete with those whose first language was English. They half tried to voice their fears, but then disguised them, and isolation increased their anxiety. Because their parents did not listen, they felt shame. They should, instead, have been proud of their effort, and have proudly tracked what they were actually achieving.

4. *Discover what her own goals are.* In the hectic daily management of life with a teenager, we may forget to explore our child's own hopes and goals. Our interest in a child's aims, however, can help her focus goals and keep her hopes alive. When a parent asks, "What do you want to make of your life?" or "What jobs do you want to have?" or "Where would you like to live or travel?" a child feels that her hopes are validated. If we know something about our teenager's long-term hopes, we will be better equipped to guide her day-to-day decisions.

If a child does her best, but cannot meet a parent's expectations, she feels isolated, out of place within the family, and often unable to find new routes to achievement. Our children need to please us, and they need us to have expectations which are attuned to their own strengths and interests. Our willingness to support them as they work toward *their* goals is an important sign of that confidence-giving love and respect.

Communicating Our Wish to Understand

For some, the teenage years can be a series of torments, and the pressures on adolescents seem to be increasing. Suicide—the most blatant of all signs of depressed self-esteem—is the second leading cause of death (accident and murder being the first) among 15- to 24-year-olds, and suicide rates have risen more than 70% since 1982. Adolescents can have huge difficulty discussing problems about food, weight, bullying, sex, school work, relationships, friends.

A fissure can appear between generations, as parents insist that they do not know how to "reach" or "get through to" a child, while a child complains that her parents do not "see" or "listen." A child exclaims, "You don't know me. You don't understand me. We have nothing to say to one another." This accusation is, in fact, a plea. The teenager wants the parent to take a new look at her, to understand this changing self, to be validated with a parent's empathy and understanding. Listening, empathizing, comforting remain important activities in parenting teenagers.

For some young people, adolescence is characterized by an intense loneliness as they realize that no one—not even a parent—can provide all they need. But we can also tell them that though we cannot cure every ill, as they may once, a very long time ago, have thought, we can offer them, through our care, the skills that will allow them to look after themselves.

We may often need to remind ourselves that a teenager does still need us, because teenagers, far more than children, are sometimes keen to disguise their need. A rough and tough exterior can cover an overwhelming sense of weakness. A brazen manner can cover increasing self-doubt. A comic, devil-may-care attitude can cover depression. Adolescents may feel so many things at once, that they do not see how to express any of them.

An adolescent may find it far easier to express her anger toward her parents than her love. She may feel more comfortable taking drastic risks than expressing fear. "Good" feelings can arouse more shame than "bad" ones. Two teenagers—Sarah, fourteen, and Patrick, fifteen—show their uneasy awareness of their inability to express who they are.

> "They go—'Show some respect!'—but I keep bouncing back, with my oh-so-jolly-exterior . . . I just string the jokes along. Sometimes I smile so hard my whole face aches, and I think anyone looking at me who knows anything about me would know that this is a facade and inside I just want to be hugged like a big kid. I swear there must be huge enormous tears in my eyes. But do they see? All they do is say, 'You just don't care. You think life's a piece of cake.' So let them think I'm like that. If they can't be bothered to take a good look, why should I spell it all out to them?"

For Sarah, her desire "to be hugged like a big kid" is covered over by the joke-cracking teenager who brings disapproval upon herself for not taking life seriously. The people who know and love her should, she believes, see through the frivolous facade. The fact that they apparently do not see through it saddens her, but she is too proud to correct them. After all, if they loved her enough, they would see her as she really is.

Patrick's parents and close friends are being pushed aside by his bravado. He sees what he is doing, yet does not know how to stop himself. "They're always on my case. Day in, day out. When they're not on at me, there's some other beef. So I scram, or go hard like steel. They *think* I'm hard. 'Nothing gets to you,' my sister keeps saying, and my Dad says, 'What does it take to get through to you?' So to them, I don't figure. Like they only see the top layer. And that's good, because underneath is more than they can handle, I guess. More than I can, anyway . . . With my friends, it's like we keep shining up that hard part, but we know what it's for."

At fifteen, Patrick is well aware that his tough exterior hides his confusion, which is intensified as his parents fail to see beyond his feigned indifference ("I scram, or go hard like steel."). He is disturbed both by his parents' dissatisfaction with him and by their "beef" or dissatisfaction with other things. He does not talk about his feelings with his friends, but believes that there is a shared understanding about the purpose of their tough manner.

Debbie, fifteen, acts "tough" because she feels misunderstood, not listened to, and interfered with. "When I see my mother coming towards me," Debbie said, "I feel her eyes boring into me. You know, it's as though she'd really like to drill holes with those eyes, and just destroy everything that's there. She won't see what I am, so—what the hell—I make it real hard for her, and make her see something that's worse than I am. I don't know what she thinks, but sometimes, I guess, she thinks I'm just what I pretend to me, and boy, does that upset me. I mean she should know better than that. She does know better than that. But sometimes she doesn't know, or isn't sure."

These teenagers feel

- isolated (because no one understands them)
- confused (because they see their inability to make themselves

understood and often wonder whether they understand themselves)

- rejected (because others' inability to hear what they are trying
to say is experienced as a rejection)

To maintain our teenager's self-esteem, we must work with them
to prevent these feelings. And, to prevent these feelings, we must
keep the lines of communication open. Often parents think they listen, think they are fostering discussion, when their children describe them otherwise. Over and over again young people insist
that parents do not understand, do not see, do not hear, do not listen. They complain that conversations are "one-sided," that parents
talk *to* them, not *with* them, and that, as a result, they "switch off."

We must listen to them, keep them switched on—both to us and
to themselves.

PARENTS CAN WORK WITH THEIR TEENAGER TO DEVELOP COMMUNICATION SKILLS.

*The first step in helping children improve their ability to communi-
cate with us and express themselves is to suppress our tendency to pass
judgment on what they say.*

Teenagers regularly cite "being judged" as the thing they dislike
most about their parents. Here are ways to avoid making them feel
"judged."

- When they tell us how they feel—unloved, perhaps, unwanted,
ignored, pressured, condemned—we can listen to their story,
and give it the validity it deserves. We do not say, "That's ridiculous!" "What nonsense!" or "You're out of your mind." A
teenager's *feelings* cannot be "ridiculous" or "nonsense." They
are felt, and therefore they are real.

We can register their feelings by naming the feeling that is expressed by what they say. When a teenager says, "I could have died!" we should say, "It was a difficult situation—you must have been embarrassed" (Not "Aren't you exaggerating?"). When a teenager says, "I was the ugliest in the room," we should say, "You felt very self-conscious" (Not "Nonsense, you weren't"). In this way, we show we are registering their feelings, and thus assure them that they are communicating with us.

- We must not (appear to) be shocked by what our teenager says.

  Expressions of disappointed surprise ("What!" or "I can't believe what I'm hearing.") are a form of "judging" what they say. We should use their different views to explore their thoughts, rather than explode them. If our teenager says that she thinks early and frequent sex is a good idea, or that it is stupid to work hard at school, we get nowhere by shutting her up. If we want to change her views, then we must maintain a dialogue with her. We can let her have her say, show some respect for the feelings or wishes behind what she says ("I see your ideas are very different from mine," "I understand that you really want to do something totally different," or "I think you have an urge to be adventurous.").

- We must listen to their very different views about people and events and movies and books and society, without condemning them. We can ask (keeping amazement and criticism out of your voice) "What is it you like about this?" "Why is she such a good friend?" or "What concerns you most about your school/your society/your future?" We can avoid saying, "How can you watch that rotten program?" "Why do listen to that awful music?" or "Isn't it about time you took some notice of the world around you?"

Teenagers want to communicate when we are willing to listen. They also want to hear, through our listening, that we understand they are independent people with their own thoughts and opinions.

Give them "verbal space" to speak. We should avoid "tag-questions" or "leading questions," which suggest that we already know the answer—or what the answer should be—to questions we put to our teenager. We should allow our teenager scope to answer for herself and ask, "What do you think of this?" "Do you like him?" and "Is that a good idea, or not?" (Not "That's a lovely dress, isn't it?" "Isn't he nice?" or "That would be good, wouldn't it?").

Adolescence is a time during which a child feels very strongly that she has her own opinions and ideas, but sometimes she has great difficulty identifying them or finding a satisfactory way of expressing them. If we lead her to an answer, then we frustrate this legitimate effort.

It is important not to show signs of impatience or irritation: Sighing and frantic gestures are experienced by the sensitive teenager as forms of punishment and will promptly put an end to her self-disclosure. The best way to let her communicate with you is to listen—by calmly receiving what she says, by not interrupting or showing impatience. Show her in some way that you have registered what she has said and then respond respectfully to what she says.

As parents we have to learn to accept criticism. A teenager is likely to be critical of some of the things we say and do. Let her voice these criticisms. We should not claim to be perfect, and we should not need to be perfect; so when our child spots our imperfections with her keen critical eye, we should not deny what she says (as in "How can you say that!" or "How dare you!"). Treat her criticisms as her way of saying, "I can see things that you do not, and I want to be different from you," which is a normal part of growth. Her criticisms are not rejections of you, but rather explorations of her different hopes or thoughts.

Remember, if you admit her ideas and opinions and feelings into your ongoing conversation or dialogue with your teenager, then you have a much better chance of sustaining the close relationship that will continue to support her self-esteem and self-confidence.

Reciprocate by telling her how you feel, rather than telling her what she is. For example, try saying "I worry when you go out dressed like that because you may attract attention you really don't want," rather than "You look like you're asking for trouble." Or try, "I think you're capable of doing really well in school. I'm worried that your friends are convincing you that hard work is uncool, or unworthwhile," rather than "You're so lazy you don't know what hard work is."

In this conversational mode, you can encourage your teenager to frame her feelings in a similar vein. When she says, "You're the worst parent in the world. No one else is forbidden to go," you might answer: "I know it's difficult not to be able to do what your friends can do" or "I know you really want to buy that jacket. It's disappointing not to be able to." In this way, you coach her to modify her accusations against you.

When your teenager is rude or unruly or rebellious, take time to ask what is bothering her. Too often, parents say "The trouble with you is . . ." or "Your problem is . . . ," when the best route to discovering that trouble is through the teenager's own account. Why not say, "You sound angry today" or "Something is clearly upsetting you," rather than, "You're so rude" or "You never listen to me." Then ask her to explain her troubles and her problems herself.

Think positive: Parents are very seldom helpless; there is virtually always some way of reaching your child. A parent has a good shot at gaining a teenager's confidence. For though I heard teenagers complain about parents not listening or understanding, they acknowledged a solid groundwork of connection and empathy.

Alongside a teenager's complaints about what a parent would or would not see, about what she could not "appreciate" or "understand," were assertions that the person who understood them most was a parent. Most girls said that their mother was the person they were most likely to confide in, the person they were most likely to bring their problems to—problems about school, friends, siblings—and sometimes, about their fathers. Most boys said that they would trust at least one parent with their confidences. Between most teenagers and parents there are pathways: We simply need the skills to make use of them.

How Sexually Maturing Bodies Impact Self-Esteem

The physical changes of adolescence—the growth spurt, the development of secondary sexual characteristics (such as the growth of body hair, the growth of breasts and widening of hips and the onset of menstruation in girls, the enlargement of the penis and testicles, and nocturnal emissions—or wet dreams—in boys)—are exciting, but they can also be confusing. Teenagers grow at different rates. Some boys of fourteen are the same size as many eleven-year-olds, and some look full grown. Accustomed to comparing themselves with peers, teenagers who are "off track," or different from most of their friends, feel odd, unsure, and excluded, however much support they have at home.

Thomas, at fourteen, said, "Each day I get to school and the guys I go around with are two inches taller. They're going to grow and grow and I'm going to be stuck down here. When we're out to-gether they talk—like they talk above me, you know, mouth to ear, with me far below them, saying, 'Hello there, remember me down here?' "

For girls the greatest problem about growth is not delayed de-velopment, which they deal with rather well, but early development. Thomas's wry humor uncovers his despair that he will never start to grow. Linda, thirteen, wanted to "run away from the new layer that's decided to attach itself to me."

Teenage girls, as they develop breasts and put on weight, may become extremely self-conscious. Some girls become too sensitive about what they *should* look like to be able to see themselves di-rectly and honestly. Young adolescent girls speak with pathos about the trials and tribulations of being a visible object in their world.

Sara, thirteen, said that when she walked into a room full of peo-ple their eyes pressed into her like barbed wires. Another girl said that even among her family—in gatherings with grandparents and aunts and uncles and cousins—when people hugged her and showed her warmth and love, she felt she had to defend herself against them. "I kind of put on a mental suit of armor. I clamp my-self in it, and then walk into the room. Grandma opens her arms up and cries "You're beautiful! Isn't she a beauty? Look at my beauty!" and I want to scream. I feel like my nipples are sticking out for everyone to see, and I can feel my thighs sticking together, and I think of little things, like whether there are any of those gooey specks of dirt between my toes. That admiration is excru-ciating! It swoops down on you. Oh, suit of armor, where are you now? How can you defend yourself against it? All those eyes on you, thinking 'Ooh, ah—hasn't the little girl gone and got all devel-oped?' An animal at a zoo gets more respect."

The most important way we can prevent a teenager's self-consciousness from dragging her self-esteem down is to help her accept her sexually maturing and changing body.

Be willing to talk about her physical development and its implications. It is crucial that a child be able to talk with you about her body, its development, and her own sexual feelings.

There is no one way to talk about these matters, and we have to be sensitive to our child's feelings. She may wish to discuss sexual matters and her sexuality and physical development with only one parent. She may be immensely shy, and feel that too much discussion is more than she can handle. Or, she may be quite willing to discuss her changing body openly and even joke about it.

If you have a hard time talking about sex—and many of us do, especially with our child—then admit it. "This is so private, that it's hard for me to talk about it, too." But use that as an opening, not a closing of the discussion.

- Find out, when she asks you something about sex or her body, what her question actually is.

   She may ask whether condoms are reliable, when her real question is whether she should give in to her boyfriend's pressure to have sex. She may ask about "stuff on her panties" when she is worried about vaginal discharge. Let her know—by looking at her, giving her time to have her say, and perhaps repeating words that seem to embarrass her—that you are willing to discuss anything with her.
- Once you understand her question, either answer it as straightforwardly and completely as you can, or help her find the answer. "I don't know what that's called, but we can ask the doctor, or look it up" is a perfectly acceptable response.

Initiate conversations about topics you think are important. It is important that teenagers have some emotional coaching in thinking about what sex means—when they are ready for it, how their part-ner might respond, and what complications there may be both physical and mental. They might not seek your advice on these mat-ters, so you may have to begin the discussion. Young people should understand that sex has great personal significance, and that many people decide it is appropriate only in the context of a very close and long-term relationship.

- Some teenagers need reminding that sex is appropriate only when both partners want to engage in it, and when each has a clear idea of what love making means to the other.
- Teenagers are often confused by desires that seem to come from nowhere. Your child might welcome discussion about the mean-ing of desire—how sometimes it can be very personal, while in some situations it is transient and means very little.
- Encourage her to distinguish between deep feelings and pass-ing fancies. Her own feelings really provide an important source of information about who she is. Whom she is attracted to is an important fact about her. Her physical feelings may be telling her something that is important about herself.
- Her body belongs to her—to care for and use according to her own desires and her own best judgment. She should never have sex, or any physical contact, simply to please someone else, or from fear of losing someone else.

This open communication about sexual activity, sexual feelings, and their implications will not, as some parents fear, make a teenager more likely to have sex. Instead, such important emotional coach-ing will give a child tools for thinking constructively about whether or not to engage in sexual activity.

Help your teenager with practical matters of hygiene. This may include the use of sanitary napkins, the good fit of a bra, the use of deodorants (and explain that these are optional), the need to wash frequently as they perspire more, the care of their skin. Take them to a doctor if they develop acne—this is not a hygiene or dieting problem, but a genetic one. It is now easily treatable, and no teenager should suffer the humiliation of severe acne.

Teenagers are still very young people, and their grooming and hygiene needs change at puberty. They need to be taught how to handle these new conditions, just as they needed your help in learning how to wash and groom themselves when they were very young children.

Stay alert to the emotional aspects of physical changes. Many young people experience marked mood swings. I have already discussed our need to tolerate a teenager's bouts of irritability and depression. A teenager is also likely to experience intense restlessness. When your teenage child needs suddenly to go out, to dance, or to throw a party because she is "bouncing off the walls doing nothing," then help her find a "steam reducing" activity. Sports are excellent for young people, but they can also go for a walk or a run, cook a complicated dish, build a cupboard, or paint a picture.

Just as disturbing as hyperactivity is the lethargy that seems to overcome teenagers, when nothing seems worthwhile. Remember, however independent she is in so many ways, she still needs you. Suggest going to a movie, or going shopping with you (even to the grocery store). Lethargy is self-reinforcing, and it is worthwhile trying to jump start a lethargic teenager. As we get her moving just a little, we can keep her going by giving her hopes a free rein ("List all the things you'd like to do and be") and then drawing a link between those hopes and her reality ("You could do, or begin to work toward doing at least one thing on the list now"). Just sitting with her and listening to her hopes and doubts can be effective—a way of reassuring her that she is *not* alone.

Teenagers Need Discipline and Respect for Their Maturity

Good parenting techniques during adolescence are not different from good parenting techniques throughout childhood. At every stage of our children's lives, we must find ways of showing our love for them, our interest in what they think, and our respect for their feelings. Every skill or technique for discipline and support that has been previously highlighted in this book can also be used with teenagers. However, as a teenager reaches toward maturity, and wants to feel like an adult, there are certain guidelines to keep in mind.

Maintain high standards of discipline

- Discipline should be accompanied by the intensive use of reasoning and explanation. This may be exhausting—teenagers are keen arguers—but reasoned arguments are essential in guiding a young person's thoughts and in maintaining your authority. Reasons do not have to be abstract or deep: reasons such as, "It's too dangerous" or "It's not convenient for us" or "You have too much school work to finish" are good enough. Without them, however, a teenager feels simply "bullied" or "dictated to" or "treated like a child."

- Make sure your child knows the rules you expect her to follow. This will avoid any plea of "innocence through ignorance." Since teenagers are such keen arguers, it is better not to give them a chance to say, "I didn't realize you wanted me home so early."

- Set up certain rules in the form of a contract. For example, a child may be allowed to stay out until a certain hour if she notifies you where she is, if you are able to contact her, or if she checks in with you. Or, she may be able to drive if she never drinks, if she doesn't have more than two people in the car with her, if she does not use the radio (and hence avoids possible distractions).

  Sometimes this contract, in which privileges and responsibilities are linked, is implicit: this means both she and you understand what standards of behavior are expected. Sometimes the contract has to be spelled out—even written out, so that there is less likely to be a dispute about your expectations and her agreement. She shows responsibility by keeping to the contract: this takes greater maturity than simply being obedient or following someone else's rules.

- Your discipline should have a close logical connection to the misdeed. Your aim, after all, is to teach a child that she has to be responsible for the consequences of her actions. When she misuses any privilege, then that privilege must be denied her until she takes definite steps to repair any wrong or damage that has resulted from her failure, or she has managed to regain your trust.

- Use encouragement for good behavior as often as possible. Trust, of course, is the best encouragement. It has practical benefits: You can give her more freedom when you trust her (when you know she will be where she says she will be, when you know she will be home at the agreed time, when you know she will remember to do what she has promised to do). A parent's trust also gives a child great emotional support.

Give teenagers a "contract of responsibility." Responsibility is not always a burden. It has many benefits. It can remind a child that she is capable, reliable, and effective.

- A teenager should be given responsibility in graded steps. She can show you that she can organize her time, manage her "finances," keep to her contracts. You can reward her for this maturity by giving her more freedom.
- Explain that her privileges are also responsibilities. Her ability to go out with her friends, or to use expensive family items (whether these are computers or cars), or make use of the home to entertain friends involves a contract of responsibility: She will be allowed out on her own if she acts sensibly and is home on time; she will be able to use family equipment if she cares for it and herself while she uses it; she can throw a party if she follows your rules about alcohol, makes sure her guests respect your belongings, and she cleans up afterward.
- Teenagers can be given responsibility for younger children. They can also be given responsibility for taking out the trash, clearing the yard, watering and cutting the grass. This will give them the experience of care and concern. As they help the family by taking on more responsibility, we can let them participate in some family decisions—about holidays, outings, menus, and meal times.

We reinforce in a teenager the importance of being accountable for her own behavior when we offer them a "contract of responsibility." A teenager's accountability for her own promises and actions is a crucial source of confidence.

Teenagers at Risk

Teenagers are often stereotyped as impulsive, and they often do act impulsively, with apparent thoughtlessness or recklessness. They are described by their parents as acting "thoughtlessly," "selfishly," with "tunnel vision." Yet adolescents themselves claim they are acting responsibly, or responsibly enough. They genuinely believe they are taking care, or taking enough care. They believe their parents are wrong to worry—because they, in their youthful confidence and youthful pride, do not see themselves at risk. Death, for teenagers, is often no more than the fiction of Huckleberry Finn's funeral: Huck is able to watch his own funeral and savour the praise heaped upon him and then to live to make mischief for many long years to come. Adolescents cannot, really, imagine themselves as dead. They are far too full of life and energy, and too excited by their new-found strength and their futures. We, as parents, want to sustain their optimism; but we also want our child to be sensible.

Teenagers take unacceptable risks for two primary reasons.

1. *Many adolescents take unacceptable risks under the influence of peer pressure.* Fearing ridicule from their peers more than the consequences of a dangerous activity, an adolescent will experiment with cocaine and designer drugs, or will drive under the influence of alcohol or drugs, or will take some part in vandalism. Pressure from peers to act destructively or simply stupidly may also come from not wanting to be left out. Some teenagers admitted that they agreed to have sex because all their friends were doing it, and they felt their innocence made them a "freak" or "real peculiar" or "the odd one out." The fear of peer rejection can be stronger than their concern for their well being.

2. *Many adolescents are intellectually unable to assess risks.* Teenagers have great mental abilities, but their ability to assess risk lags far behind other mental developments. They retain something of the five-year-old's response: "See, Mom and Dad,

I can cross the road myself without getting killed." If a teenager has done something a few times without detrimental consequences, then she may believe it is safe. Or, if she has seen a friend do something—take drugs, drive under the influence of alcohol, have intercourse without using contraception—she may think that because others do it without coming to harm, then it is safe or safe enough.

Teenagers tend to greatly overestimate how many of their friends are having sex "safely" or using drugs "without having problems" or smoking "without becoming addicted." These young people may have access to reliable figures about pregnancy, addiction, or cancer, but they believe that they will be the exception.

COMMUNICATING CAUTION TO OUR TEENAGER

We face an uphill struggle enabling our adolescent children—who believe they will never grow old and will never die—to understand what risks they are actually taking when they smoke, when they try drugs, when they drive, when they have sex. This is another important reason we must keep the lines of communication with our teenager open and, at the same time, sustain our parental authority. We must find ways to reach an adolescent whose maturity tends to be uneven and patchy.

We must educate our child about the risks she takes with drugs, with sex, with cars or motorbikes. Never assume a child "knows" something until you tell her and she shows she understands.

If you are concerned about specific behavior that puts her at risk— for example, of addiction, accidents, pregnancy, disease, or severe unhappiness—make sure you voice your concerns. **Engage in a**

structured conversation: neither occasional nor constant nagging will be as effective as a structured discussion.

- *Explain that you are worried, and explain why.*

  It is useful to express your fears in terms of your personal outlook. So it is more effective to say, "I'm worried that you are becoming far too involved with a boy/girlfriend," than it is to say, "If a girl as young as you thinks she's in love, she can ruin her future," or "If you keep mooning over her, your grades will go down the tubes." A teenager is likely to respond to your personal concern; she is also likely to dismiss your predictions.

- *Discuss possible outcomes of her behavior, how severe they would be, and how much she would lose.*

  Seek her input as you discuss the possible consequences of her behavior. You could coach her to think more carefully about such consequences by asking, "Where do you see this relationship going?" and then, "What might that mean to your hopes for going to college?" If you think the scenario she describes is utterly unrealistic, it is more effective to say, "I find that simplistic and unrealistic." Try to avoid saying, "That's ridiculous" or "You don't know what you're talking about." After all, you want to keep those lines of communication open, but ridicule and rejection may close them down.

- *Make sure she takes in the information you want to give her—but make sure you give your child the chance to speak, too.*

  It can be irritating and humiliating to be silenced by someone walking out of a room, or hanging up a telephone receiver, or simply interrupting and shouting. Explain that this conversation may be difficult because you care so much about her. Show that you agree not to shout at or interrupt her, and to stay put until the conversation has come to a (temporary) end, and you ask the same respect from her.

To make sure you have successfully communicated the information you want—about the risk of pregnancy, disease, addiction, or the consequences of lowering her school grades—ask her to repeat the important points. "It's often difficult getting information across," you could explain. "I just want to make sure I've managed to make my point."

If your teenager insists that she cannot give up certain friends, or activities, which seem more dangerous than you'd like, but are borderline acceptable, then suggest ways of making her behavior safer. The tone of the discussion should be one of two people drawing up a contract: "How can we together come up with a means of your doing with reasonable safety what you most want to do?"

One common issue of safety involves the use of a car, and this can be made safer if it is agreed she will only accept a lift (or drive herself) when not more than three people are in the car, that the radio will be off, that there will be no drinking on the evening of using the car, that there will be no speeding. The privilege can be granted only in the context of that safety contract.

Such a safety contract could also apply to a teenager staying at home while you are out of town. Ask her what she is worried about (so that your fears are not the only ones to be answered).

Some behavior, of course, can be simply classified as too dangerous, and therefore, unacceptable.

• *Drugs are always dangerous. No one can "handle" them.*

One difficulty is that the use of drugs can cloud judgment. A teenager may deny she has a problem, and she may well believe this herself. If you discover a child does use drugs, then seek professional help. Your child may need to go into a program or, at the very least, will need counselling.

- *If she is sexually active, then practicing safe sex is a must—not a matter to be assessed by individual judgment.*

    If a teenager understands the true risk involved, then she is very likely to take reasonable steps to protect herself. The great difficulty many parents have is convincing a teenager that the risks she hears about are real—and that they really apply to her. You may have to engage in many structured conversations, whereby you express your fears, make sure she listens and takes in the information you want her to have.

- *The separation of drinking and driving is also nonnegotiable.*

    This is an essential part of that "contract" whereby privileges are linked to responsibilities: She cannot drive with anyone who has had anything alcoholic to drink. When the contract is broken, the privilege is denied.

Adolescent children probably will exercise poor judgment somewhere along the line, but *we should stand by them, and assure them of their personal value—to us and to themselves*—even when their behavior distresses us. "I'm upset and hurt at how you have behaved," we can say, clearly and firmly. Then we can help them learn from their mistakes as they repair the damage they have done to our trust. This repair work should not be too difficult. A child needs our trust if she is to preserve her own confidence. The graded steps toward privilege and responsibility, whereby a teenager shows her ability to be reliable and effective, may be climbed again.

Often parents hear about the importance of letting go of their teenage children. We may be warned about being overprotective or undermining their need to be their own person as we watch out for them, argue with them, and plead with them to continue to care for themselves. But teenagers need our support as they experience their own physical development and a range of new desires and pressures. They need a parent's listening attention as they express their fluctuating thoughts and feelings. They need a parent's loving appreciation as they suffer from their own sense of awkwardness and self doubt. If we are to sustain their confidence through the teenage years, we must not let go too quickly.

ten

Raising Moral Children

L ike Marmee in *Little Women,* we wish we could offer our children a fairer world: Given our limited power, we nonetheless hope that we will raise them to make the world a better place. To do so, we have to raise children who are caring, socially responsible, fair-minded, and respectful of others. In this final chapter, I deal with the awesome question: "How can we raise children who will improve the world?" or "How do we raise children who are good?" The methods by which we raise moral children are the very methods by which we raise a confident child: So the guidelines already set out in this book also allow us to do the important job of raising moral children.

There are four "mind sets" closely linked to moral behavior:

1. care for the welfare of others
2. responsibility for one's actions
3. concern for the quality of one's own conduct
4. understanding of justice

As we teach our children to be moral, we do not necessarily teach them what choices to make, but we do teach them to be aware that they will have to make choices—sometimes difficult ones. We teach them that they are then responsible for what they do, and we hope to give them the tools to think about their behavior and assess its consequences. If we coach them in acquiring skills to reflect upon the consequences of their behavior and to change their behavior to get the results they want, we give them the power to be responsible for their behavior. If we coach them to develop emotional intelligence, we give them the capacity to understand their own feelings and the feelings of others. Through this understanding they can understand others' needs and acquire the tools to care for others. This chapter looks more closely at how the skills we instill for confidence can be adapted to guide a child to moral maturity.

Nurturing Empathy

Empathy involves a strong awareness of other people's feelings and some understanding of why people feel what they do. Even very young children have a capacity for empathy. Infants as young as three months old show distress when another baby cries. Very young children observe people responding to other people's feelings, and they then acquire what is called a "repertoire of sensitive responses," or a set of tools for responding to others, as they come to recognize that people in different circumstances require different responses.

Children are eager psychologists: They intently observe the people around them, and they constantly try to make sense of changing voices, faces, and moods. But the world of human feeling is incredibly complex, and even the most astute child can use a parent's help. Empathy needs to be developed.

- As parents, we can encourage empathy by saying what we feel, and why. We can educate a child's emotions by talking about feelings and increasing her awareness of them. We can say: "I'm angry because everyone is asking me something at once." "I'm worried because your brother in feeling unwell." "The baby is watching you. She's very interested in what you're doing!" "That must have been disappointing for you." This kind of conversation extends her emotional vocabulary.

- We can coach our child to understand others' feelings. We can ask, "Why do you think your brother wanted to hit you?" or "Why does he refuse to play with you when his friends are with him?" This emotional coaching helps her understand how and why certain emotions arise.

- We can use emotional coaching as we explain why certain behavior is unacceptable: "Don't hold it: he's worried you'll take it from him." "Don't push her away. She's trying to help." This helps a child acquire the skill to distinguish between her response to a situation and someone else's response. She is then able to understand what her behavior may mean to someone else.

- We can help a child manage her own feelings. When we say, "I see that you are angry, but that doesn't mean you can hit your brother," we acknowledge her feelings, but insist that she find an appropriate way of expressing them. As we help her distinguish between what she feels and what she does, she is better equipped to identify an appropriate way of expressing what she feels.

Nurturing Responsibility

The next step to moral guidance is responsibility. Though the ability to take responsibility for what one does involves emotional control and maturity, a child senses something good or bad within herself from a very early age.

Guilt is a very early emotion, and it is important in regulating the quality of relationships with others. It arises as a child understands that she is someone who does things and that what she does has consequences. She can knock something with her arm and it spills. She can bump into something and it breaks. She can hit someone and he cries. She learns, too, that people may have strong responses to what she does. Some of the things she does are rewarded, and others are punished.

Guilt can become torment when a child feels that she is "bad" and unable to improve; but when a child's behavior is the target of criticism (not the child herself), and when she learns that she can control her behavior, make amends when something goes wrong, and avoid similar mishaps or mistakes in the future, then that early sense of guilt becomes a positive source of responsibility. Guidelines for teaching a child to take responsibility for her actions are given throughout this book—but most specifically in the chapters that deal with problem-solving skills. Here is a recap of how we coach a child to be responsible for what she does:

- Identify her role in both behavior you approve of and behavior you disapprove of. When she achieves something, remark on how her effort or concentration or practice helped her achieve what she did. When she quarrels, or breaks something, or in any other way "messes up," encourage her to identify her own contribution to the mishap (even if it is not solely her "fault"). In this way, a child will come to see herself as an agent—someone who acted voluntarily and whose actions have consequences.

- Encourage her to think up a range of possible actions. Whether she has a problem with her sister or with a friend, or she is simply bored, we can exercise her mind by suggesting that she come up with various ideas about how to solve problems or what to do. In this way, she will experience herself as having choices.
- Ask her to talk or think through the consequences of her behavior before she acts—especially when she is trying to solve a problem with a brother, sister, or friend. In this way, she will gain skills in assessing her behavior and develop greater control over her choices because she can think about possible consequences.
- When she decides what to do, ask her to assess the results of her behavior. This skill will help her track the actual consequences of her behavior.

Whether she is thinking about improving her performance in basketball, making friends, or ending a dispute with her brother, this pattern of reflection—involving awareness of herself as a person whose actions make a difference, who can choose how to act, and who can change how she behaves—lays the groundwork, too, of moral responsibility.

Concern for One's Own Conduct

Caring about one's conduct is the crux of confidence. A child who cares about herself will care about what she does and how she affects others. The logical outcome of true self-esteem is concern for oneself *and* others. This book as a whole is directed toward increasing our parenting abilities on this score. As we help a child understand others' feelings, as we help her see how her behavior affects others, as we help her experience her power to solve problems, she gains confidence in her positive impact on the world around her. This confidence involves concern for her behavior, and the ability to assess her behavior and to keep trying until she gets the results she wants. Here are a few guidelines to highlight:

- *We maintain belief in our child's basic goodness, even when we criticize her behavior.* By criticizing a child's behavior, rather than the child herself (methods described in Chapter 5), we keep alive her faith in her basic goodness. When we help her improve her behavior, we show we have high expectations of her.
- *We foster a free exchange of ideas.* Throughout this book I have emphasized the importance of listening to children and not punishing them (through ridicule, derision, withholding of love) for their ideas and thoughts. When a child feels that her own ideas are tolerated, she will be more tolerant of others. Psychologists have found that it is children with low self-esteem who are most intolerant of others. Devaluing others—through mockery, suspicion, and prejudice—is an attempt to retain some vestige of self-worth when one feels one cannot be positively effective oneself. Self-esteem abolishes the need for negative defenses against others.
- *We encourage our child to speak her mind.* When we listen to a child, we encourage her to say what she thinks. We listen effectively as we give her our attention and show respect for her feelings (though we may disagree with her opinions). (Effective listening techniques are described in Chapters 3, 4, and 9). This habit of mind is essential to the ability to stand by one's principles.
- *We encourage her to internalize rules and values.* As we discipline her positively, in the authoritative style described in Chapter 5, we set down guidelines for behavior and explain the reasons be-

hind our rules. As we explain our rules to her, she comes to understand the logic of our rules. She then has the tools to judge
her behavior herself. When she is able to think before she acts
and assess the possible consequences of her actions—as we can
coach her to do—then she can also trust her own judgment.

Understanding of Justice

Though justice is a difficult concept, children are naturally drawn
to think about it. Different people will have very different ideas
about what is just. "That's not fair!" is a cry we often hear, but as a
child makes this protest, she may be using it as a version of "I don't
like this!" However, children do seem to have a strong desire for
things to be "fair," and as we try to be fair to our child, we help develop her understanding of justice, and coach her away from this
(often selfish) viewpoint of fairness being what she wants, to an
awareness of her interdependence with others. Our aim should not
be to raise a child who will always come up with a "right" answer
to the question "What is just?" but a child who is able to think
about issues of fairness and need, who can consider other people
when she decides what to do, and who can link her *thoughts* about
justice to her *behavior.*

- To understand justice, a child needs empathy. We help extend
  our child's understanding of justice as we encourage her to think
  about others' views and others' feelings. As we engage in emotional coaching, and help her to care for the welfare of others,
  we also increase her understanding of justice. Someone who
  does not understand others' thoughts and feelings cannot understand how to treat others fairly.
- Our style of discipline plays an important role in a child's understanding of justice. As we follow the guidelines for an au-

thoritative style of discipline, in which we explain rules to our child, discuss the reasons for these rules, and are as consistent as possible in adhering to these rules, we provide our child with the framework to think about right and wrong, and to reason about right and wrong. Instead of saying "Do this because I say so and I'm boss," we can, often enough, say "You must follow this rule because the rule is, most of the time, better for everyone." Sometimes these rules involve the safety of the child or of others (for example: "You can only ride on a bike path"). Sometimes rules are made for the convenience of the family as a whole (for example: "You have to be home in time to help prepare dinner"). Sometimes the rules are linked to religious beliefs or practices (for example: "You have to get your homework done before sundown, so you can observe the Sabbath"). Sometimes the rules are linked to concern for the environment ("You have to walk if it's less that two miles"). The important thing is that rules are seen as supported by good reasons.

We offer a model of justice as we discipline our children in ways that make sense to them: If a child is able to understand our rules and discipline, she will be able to think more carefully about an action and its consequences.

• We offer a model of justice (however small scale) as we take into account different people's needs in our own behavior. We can explain that we have to leave the swimming pool because a younger sister is tired, or we have to be quiet so another child can study, but that a longer swimming time and a noisy period can be enjoyed in the future, or has been enjoyed in the recent past.

Knowledge of others' needs will be increased through her experience of her peers. Chapter 8 sets out guidelines for enhancing a child's experiences with her friends by coaching her toward a wider emotional understanding of others and an ability to solve interpersonal problems.

- As we teach our child that her behavior can have positive consequences, she can be inspired to improve her society. Many children feel outraged by unfairness to others. This outrage can turn into frustration and depression if they believe they cannot do anything to improve their own lives; but if they learn that they have the power to change things around them, then this outrage can become a positive source of action. (Guidelines for helping a child experience the positive impact of her behavior are given in Chapters 4, 5, 6 and 8.)

Back to Basics:
Getting to Know Your Child

No parenting book can give the most important information we need to help our child attain confidence for life. We need to understand her emotional needs for our companionship, our affection, and our attention. We need to help her discover her abilities and to guide her toward fulfilling her potential. We need to assess her energy and help direct it. We need to be aware of her fears and help soothe them. The only source of information for all these is the child herself, and we can only obtain this information if we keep the lines between us and our child open.

For all its daily urgency, parenthood is often a series of half-spoken dialogues: The child knows the parent loves and cares, yet never how, and how much. From the parents' perspective, the love for a child is so overwhelming that it seems enough—yet because it is overwhelming, there is always more to give. From the child's perspective, however, this love contains gaps and flaws. A child may complain that we do not "see" or "hear" or "understand." A child believes we give more to a sibling or stepchild, to our partner or friends, to our career or our politics. When a child's dissatisfaction begins to show—especially in her loss of self-esteem—we feel shocked, offended, and confused. "What have I not done right? Why is my best so far from enough?" we ask. Sometimes our child seems to want so much from us that we find her "unreasonable" or "spoiled." Our child may be making continuous demands because what we give her is not quite right.

To be the parent she needs, we have to understand her needs. Some of her most pressing needs are to acquire skills to develop her potential abilities, set and meet high standards for her behavior, and find ways of interacting positively with people around her. Our child needs our help in acquiring the skills that will enable her to value herself and care for her future.

Growing up is not easy, and we cannot pretend, to ourselves or our children, that we can make it so. Our children will grow up in an increasingly unstable environment, with chronic relationship breakdown and uncertainty about jobs. But they will also grow up with good health and unprecedented freedoms to control their lives in terms of work, relationships, lifestyles, and beliefs. The great challenge of both insecurity and freedom, instability and opportunity, can be met only by children who have the skills to put forth effort, assess their behavior, and engage responsibly with their society. We cannot afford to disguise from them the real quality of their performance by praising them constantly, for whatever they do, or for just being themselves. The social critic Christopher Lasch warned, "Children need to risk failure and disappointment, to overcome obstacles, to face down the terrors that surround them. Self respect cannot be conferred; it has to be earned." The purpose of this book is to offer parents guidelines to help their children earn the confidence they need to make the best of their lives.

References

Thomas Achenbach and Catherine Howell, "Are America's children's problems getting worse? A 13-year comparison." *Journal of the American Academy of Child and Adoelscent Psychiatry,* November, 1989.

N. Albert and A. T. Beck, "Incidence of depression in early adolescence: A preliminary study." *Journal of Youth and Adolescence, 4,* 1975.

Terri Apter, *Altered Loves: Mothers and Daughters during Adolescence.* New York: St Martin's, 1990.

Diana Baumrind, *Familial Antecedents of Social Competence in Middle Childhood,* in press.

J. Bempechat, P. London, and C. Dweck, "Children's conceptions of ability in major domains: An interview and experimental study." *Child Study Journal, 21,* 1991.

T. Berry Brazelton, *Head Start: The Emotional Foundations of School Readiness.* Arlington, VA: National Center for Clinical Infant Programs, 1992.

J. Brophy and T. Good, "Teacher behavior and student achievement." In M. Wittrock, ed., *Handbook of Research on Teaching,* third edition. New York: Macmillan, 1986.

A. Burnett, *Youth Survey: An Analysis.* Palo Alto, CA: Palo Alto Youth Council, 1990–1.

Kim Chernin, *In My Mother's House.* New York: Ticknor and Fields, 1983.

Julie Cohen, "Mental illness among children jumps 50%." *The Sunday Times (London),* section 1, 19 March, 1995.

Stanley Coopersmith, *The Antecedents of Self-Esteem,* second edition. Palo Alto, CA: Consulting Psychologists Press, 1981.

Mihaly Csikszentmihalyi, "Play and intrinsic rewards." *Journal of Humanistic Psychology, vol.15,* no.3, 1975.

William Damon, *Greater Expectations: Overcoming the Culture of Indulgence in America's Homes and Schools.* New York: Free Press, 1995.

Judy Dunn, *Beginnings of Social Understanding.* Oxford: Basil Blackwood, 1988.

Judy Dunn and Jane Brown, "Relationships, talk about feelings and the development of affect regulation in early childhood." In J. Garber and K. A. Dodge, eds., *The Development of Emotion Regulation and Dysregulation.* Cambridge: Cambridge University Press, 1991.

Judy Dunn, "Children as psychologists: The later correlates of individual differences in understanding of emotions and other minds." In Judy Dunn, ed., *Connections between Emotion and Understanding in Development.* Hillsdale, NJ: Lawrence Erlbaum, 1995.

M. J. Elias, ed., *Social Decision-Making in the Middle School.* Gaithersburg, MD: Aspen Publishers, 1992.

J. K. Felsman and G. E. Vaillant, "Resilient children as adults: A 40-year study." In E. J. Anderson and B. J. Cohler, eds., *The Invulnerable Child.* New York: Guildford Press, 1987.

W. Fredrich, R. Reams, and J. Jacobs, "Depression and suicidal ideation in early adolescents." *Journal of Youth and Adolescence, 11,* 1982.

Haim Ginott, *Between Parent and Child.* New York: Avon, 1959.

Haim Ginott, *Between Parent and Teenager.* New York: Avon, 1971.

Haim Ginott, *Teacher and Child.* New York: Avon, 1975.

Daniel Goleman, "What do children fear most? Their answers are surprising." *New York Times,* Health, March 17, 1988.

Daniel Goleman, *Emotional Intelligence.* London: Bloomsbury, 1996.

Ian Goodyer, ed., *Mood Disorders in Childhood and Adolescence.* Cambridge: Cambridge University Press, 1994.

Ian Goodyer, ed., *The Depressed Child and Adolescent.* Cambridge: Cambridge University Press, 1995.

John Gottman and Lynn Fainsilber, "The effects of marital discord on young children's peer interaction and health." *Developmental Psychology, 25,* 1989.

John Gottman and John Parker, eds., *Conversations of Friends.* New York, Cambridge University Press, 1986.

Jean Gross, *Psychology and Parenthood.* Milton Keynes: Open University Press, 1989.

Peter Gurney, *Self-Esteem in Children with Special Educational Needs.* London: Routledge, 1988.

J. David Hawkins et. al., *Communities That Care.* San Francisco: Jossey Bass, 1992.

David Hamburg, *Today's Children: Creating a Future for a Generation in Crisis.* New York: Times Books, 1992.

Carole Hooven, John Gottman, and Lynn Fainsilber Katz, "Parental meta-emotion structure predicts family and child outcomes." In Judy Dunn, ed., *Connections between Emotion and Understanding in Development.* Hillsdale, NJ: Lawrence Erlbaum, 1995.

Martin L. Hoffman, "Empathy, social cognition and moral action." In W. Kurtines and J. Gerwitz, eds., *Moral Behavior and Development Advances in Theory, Research and Applications.* New York: John Wiley, 1984.

John Holt, *How Children Fail*. New York: Pitman, 1965.

John Hunsley, "Internal dialogue during academic examinations." *Cognitive Therapy and Research,* December, 1987.

Deborah Jackson, *Do Not Disturb: Giving Our Children Room to Grow.* London: Bloomsbury, 1993.

Ruthellen Josselson, *Finding Herself: Pathways to Identity Development in Women.* San Francisco: Jossey-Bass, 1987.

B. Keogh, C. Cahill, and D. Macmillan, "Perception of interruption by educationally handicapped children." *American Journal of Mental Deficiency, 77,* 107–108, 1972.

D. Macmillan, B. Keogh, and R. Jones, "Special education research on mildly handicapped learners." In M. Wittrock, ed., *Handbook of Research on Teaching,* third edition. New York: Macmillan, 1986.

Richard Metzger et al., "Worry changes decision-making: The effects of negative thoughts on cognitive processing." *Journal of Clinical Psychology,* January, 1990.

Tracy Kidder, *Among Schoolchildren*. Boston: Houghton Mifflin Co., 1989.

Francine Klagsbrun, *Mixed Feelings*. New York: Bantam, 1992.

Heinz Kohut, *The Analysis of the Self.* New York: International Universities Press, 1971.

Edith Neisser, *Brothers and Sisters*. New York: Harper and Row, 1951.

Joyce Carol Oates, *Foxfire*. New York: Dutton, 1993

Gerald Patterson, *Coercive Family Process*. Eugene, Oregon: Castalia, 1982.

P. Phelan, H. Yu, and A. Davidson, "Navigating the psychosocial pressures of adolescence: The voices and experiences of high school youth." *American Educational Research Journal, vol. 31,* no. 2., 1994.

Joy Pollock and Elisabeth Waller, *Day-to-Day Dyslexia*. London and New York: Routledge, 1994.

G. Pugh, E. De'Ath, and C. Smith, *Confident Parents, Confident Children: Policy and Practice in Parent Education and Support.* London: National Children's Bureau, 1994.

M. Rutter, B. Maughan, B. Mortimore, and J. Ouston, *Fifteen Thousand Hours: Secondary Schools and Their Effects on Children,* London: Open Books, 1979.

Michael Rutter and David Smith, eds., *Psychosocial Disorders in Young People.* Chichester: John Wiley, 1995.

Carol Saarni, "Emotional competence: How emotions and relationships become integrated." In R. A. Thompson, ed., *Socioemotional Development/Nebraska Symposium on Motivation, 36,* 1990.

Bettina Seipp, "Anxiety and academic analysis: A meta-analysis." *Anxiety Research, 4,* 1, 1994.

Martin Seligman, *Learned Optimism.* New York: Knopf, 1991.

Myrna Shure and George Spivack, "Interpersonal cognitive problem solving." In *14 Ounces of Preventing: A Casebook for Practitioners,* edited by R. H. Price, E. L. Cowen, R. P. Lorion, and J. Ramos-McKay. Washington D.C.: American Psychological Association, 1988.

Social Trends 1995. London: HMSO, 1995.

Daniel Stern, *The Interpersonal World of the Infant: A View from Psychoanalysis and Developmental Psychology.* New York: Basic Books, 1985.

H. Stevenson and S. Lee, *Contexts of Achievement.* Monographs for the Society for Research in Child Development, *1–2,* 1990.

Robin Stillwell, *Social Relationships in Primary School Children as Seen by Children, Mothers and Teachers.* Unpublished Ph.D. dissertation, University of Cambridge, 1984.

K. Sylva, "School influences on children's development." *Journal of Child Psychology and Psychiatry, vol. 35,* no. 1, 1991.

The Sunday Times (London), Style, "Family life: Child of divorce; 'Torn between them' by 'Anna'," 25 September, 1994.

Carol Tavris, *Anger: The Misunderstood Emotion.* New York: Simon and Schuster, 1982.

George Vaillant, *Adaptation to Life.* Boston: Little, Brown, 1977.

Judith Viorst, *Necessary Losses.* New York: Ballantine, 1986.

Janet Walker, *The Cost of Communication Breakdown.* British Telecom
    Publication, London: Burson-Marsteller, January 1995.

John Weiss, et.al., "Control-related beliefs and self-reported depressive
    symptoms in late childhood." *Journal of Abnormal Psychology, 102,*
    1993.

Index

boisterousness, 35, 116
Brown, Lyn Mikel, 22
building block game, 13–16
bullying, 33, 56, 57, 58, 108, 193, 197,
    203
  lack of confidence and, 33
  peer pressure as form of, 195
  racism as, 206
  sexual harassment as, 216

challenges, 36–37, 47, 66, 131, 137, 149
children:
  accident-prone, 32, 64, 94
  ambiguity and, 32
  anger of, 57–61, 74, 75, 76, 106, 113,
      122, 133, 222
  birth order of, 167–71
  cheering up, 62, 69
  comforting by, 87
  cruelty of, 59
  cunning of, 119
  death of, 84
  depression in, 61
  early sexual development of, 229
  empathy and, 243–44
  exceptional, 150–57
  fantasies of, 30, 38
  isolated, 180
  learning disabled, 150–53
  listening to, 59–60
  middle, 169–70
  moral development in, 19, 22
  and need for control, 21, 43, 65–66,
      114, 126
  and need for understanding, 58, 60, 71
  newness and, 31, 37, 38
  nurturing responsibility in, 245–46
  older, 167–68
  over-protectiveness and, 90–95
  parental anger and, 73–78, 79
  parent's depression and, 82–87
  "perfect," 166
  with physical disabilities, 151
  respect by, 56–57, 72, 104

respect for, 82, 97–98, 104, 111, 112,
    115, 128
silencing of, 56–57, 59
"territory" of, 194
thoughtlessness and, 104
true abilities not confronted by,
    38–39
twin, 170–71
younger, 168–69
clowning, 36, 76, 116, 117
clumsiness, 32, 131
"coldness," 57, 58, 83
communication, 221–28
  with adolescents, 221–28, 237–39
  with angry children, 57, 58–61
  emotional intelligence and, 43, 101
  judgments and, 224–25
  listening in, 225–27
  parental love and, 222–23
  between parents and children, 21–22,
      80–82, 108
  regarding risk-taking, 237–40
  sexual maturation and, 229–31
  structured conversations and, 237–40
compassion, 57
competence, 88, 89, 91, 94
  parental, 100
competition, 17, 18, 136, 156
  within the family, 21
  inevitability of, 16
  at school, 131
compliance, 93
compliments, 68, 132
concentration, 44, 65, 114
confidence, 17, 18
  in classroom, 143–47
  and concern for one's own conduct,
      246–47
  development of, 23, 53, 69, 126
  false, 29
  fluctuations in, 27
  social competence and, 33
  and tolerance for frustration, 37
  see also self-confidence

in school, 21, 143–45
    suicide and, 145
hygiene, 231–32

identity:
    friendships and, 191–93
    parents' investment in, 52–53, 77
    relinquishing of, 193–95
    "identity environment," 191
impulsiveness, 36, 45, 103, 110
    depression and, 62–63
inadequacy, sense of, 38, 39, 44, 53, 64
independence, 40, 89, 90
inferiority, sense of, 31
initiative, 54
    lack of, 34, 40, 110
instructions, 113–14, 118, 150, 155, 181
    open-ended, 48, 49
intelligence, 17, 131, 132, 154
    emotional, 18, 20, 22, 43, 70, 87,
        100–101, 243
interpersonal skills, 42, 47, 48, 180–90
inventiveness, 60

Jossleson, Ruthellen, 100
judgment, 54, 94, 131
    bad, 126
    development of, 104, 105, 110, 111,
        112, 114, 118, 128, 132
    of intelligence and ability, 131–32
    lack of confidence and, 32, 34, 36, 46
    lack of trust in, 35, 36, 46, 47
justice, understanding of, 248–50

Keaton, Diane, 148
Kidder, Tracy, 116, 156
Kramer vs. Kramer (film), 90

Lasch, Christopher, 251
laziness, 56, 108, 153, 164
leadership, 34, 46
learning:
    attitude toward, 129
    behavioral problems and, 156–57

exceptional children and, 150–57
frustration and, 37, 155
goals, 130, 132
humiliation and, 147
rates of, 150
learning disabilities, 150–55
listening, 69
    to adolescents, 225–26
    to children, 59–60
    healing power of, 69, 81
Little Women (Alcott), 242
lying, 31, 64, 75, 107, 108

marriage, failed, 95–101
    see also divorce
mental block, 30, 144–45
    anxiety and, 44
mistakes, 37, 43
    failure and, 146
    as feedback, 45, 48
    unlearning fear of, 54
money, 80, 99
moodiness, 55, 64
    of adolescents, 216–17, 232
    of parents, 72, 82, 87
moral behavior, 242–51
    concern for one's own conduct and,
        246–48
    empathy and, 243–44, 248
    guilt and, 245
    internalizing rules, values and, 247–48
    justice and, 248–50
    nurturing responsibility and, 245–46
    parent-child relationship and, 250–51
motivation:
    adolescents and, 217–18
    lack of, 38, 44, 95, 110, 111, 133
    success, failure and, 138
    unrealistic praise and, 133

nagging, 77, 107, 120
negative self-attitude, see self-esteem,
    low
newness, 31, 37, 38, 47, 50

Oates, Joyce Carol, 143
Oregon Social Learning Center, 22
Other Women (Alther), 88
over-protectiveness, 73, 90–95
   self-esteem and, 88, 91
   twelve- to fifteen-year-olds and, 92–95

panic, 47, 48
parents, parenting, 29, 71–101
   adolescent's criticism of, 226–27
   ambitions of, for children, 54, 148
   anger of, toward children, 27–28, 44,
      45, 50, 52, 53, 55, 58, 59, 69, 71,
      73–82, 108, 113, 120
   anxious children and, 44–52, 54–55
   attention to children by, 60, 61, 69, 86,
      160
   authoritarian, 110, 111, 119
   authoritative, 112, 119–20
   child's anger at, 57–61, 74, 75, 76, 106,
      113, 122, 133
   child's avoidance of, 76, 77, 80
   child's rejection of, 53, 80, 132
   and coping with child's peer pressure,
      195–96
   death of, 85, 172
   depression and, 73, 82–87
   disappointment and, 73, 77, 85, 218
   expectations of, 47, 55, 126, 127, 163,
      166–67, 217–21
   frustration of, 55, 71, 73, 77
   ideas about, 71–72, 85, 101
   identity invested in children by, 52–53, 77
   impatience of, 55, 71
   inevitable imperfections of, 20–21, 70
   moodiness and, 72, 82, 87
   over-protection by, 73, 88–95
   permissive, 110–12
   personal relationships of, 72, 73
   power struggles and, 106, 120
   self-control and, 52, 53–54, 70, 72
   sibling quarrels and, 172–74
   stress and, 72, 73, 77, 78, 80
   temperament of, 73

Patterson, Gerald, 22
peer pressure, 195
   achievement vs. belonging and,
      207–8
   as bullying, 195
   cultural, educational transitions and,
      207–8
   friendship and, 195–97
   resisting of, 196–97
   risk taking and, 236
   teasing and, 196–97
peers:
   aggressiveness toward, 56, 58, 188
   bossy, 40
   child's perception of, 135
   dependence on, 34, 40
   derogatory remarks about, 36
   envy of, 64–65, 68
   high status, 34
   inappropriate behavior with, 35
   indifference toward, 57
   lagging behind, 137
   positive impact among, 34, 186
   shyness with, 33, 47, 200
   see also friends, friendships
"perfect child," 166
perfectionism, 50
performance:
   indifference to, 55
   parental response to child's, 52, 53,
      132–35
   self-esteem and, 18, 50
   standards of, 130, 132–35, 151
permissiveness, 110–12, 119
persistence, 38, 51, 63, 132
pets, 86
   boasting about, 36
   death of, 61
Phalen, Patricia, 207–8
play structures, 89, 90–91
Pollock, Joy, 157
positive feedback, 34, 44, 51
power, 97, 122
   discovering sense of, 66

in school, 21, 143–45
  suicide and, 145
hygiene, 231–32

identity:
  friendships and, 191–93
  parents' investment in, 52–53, 77
  relinquishing of, 193–95
  "identity environment," 191
impulsiveness, 36, 45, 103, 110
  depression and, 62–63
inadequacy, sense of, 38, 39, 44, 53, 64
independence, 40, 89, 90
inferiority, sense of, 31
initiative, 54
  lack of, 34, 40, 110
instructions, 113–14, 118, 150, 155, 181
  open-ended, 48, 49
intelligence, 17, 131, 132, 154
  emotional, 18, 20, 22, 43, 70, 87,
    100–101, 243
interpersonal skills, 42, 47, 48, 180–90
inventiveness, 60

Jossleson, Ruthellen, 100
judgment, 54, 94, 131
  bad, 126
  development of, 104, 105, 110, 111,
    112, 114, 118, 128, 132
  of intelligence and ability, 131–32
  lack of confidence and, 32, 34, 36, 46
  lack of trust in, 35, 36, 46, 47
justice, understanding of, 248–50

Keaton, Diane, 148
Kidder, Tracy, 116, 156
Kramer vs. Kramer (film), 90

Lasch, Christopher, 251
laziness, 56, 108, 153, 164
leadership, 34, 46
learning:
  attitude toward, 129
  behavioral problems and, 156–57

exceptional children and, 150–57
frustration and, 37, 155
goals, 130, 132
humiliation and, 147
rates of, 150
learning disabilities, 150–55
listening, 69
  to adolescents, 225–26
  to children, 59–60
  healing power of, 69, 81
Little Women (Alcott), 242
lying, 31, 64, 75, 107, 108

marriage, failed, 95–101
  see also divorce
mental block, 30, 144–45
  anxiety and, 44
mistakes, 37, 43
  failure and, 146
  as feedback, 45, 48
  unlearning fear of, 54
money, 80, 99
moodiness, 55, 64
  of adolescents, 216–17, 232
  of parents, 72, 82, 87
moral behavior, 242–51
  concern for one's own conduct and,
    246–48
  empathy and, 243–44, 248
  guilt and, 245
  internalizing rules, values and, 247–48
  justice and, 248–50
  nurturing responsibility and, 245–46
  parent-child relationship and, 250–51
motivation:
  adolescents and, 217–18
  lack of, 38, 44, 95, 110, 111, 133
  success, failure and, 138
  unrealistic praise and, 133

nagging, 77, 107, 120
negative self-attitude, see self-esteem,
  low
newness, 31, 37, 38, 47, 50

depression and, 18–19, 61–70, 213–14
destructiveness as result of, 18–19
devaluing others and, 247
divorce and, 95–96, 97
and inability to understand others, 34, 35
overcoming, 42–70
permissiveness and, 112·
and response to success and failure, 39–40
school and, 36–40
as self-reinforcing system, 35, 37, 42
shyness and, 33
social isolation and, 35, 179–80
self-expectations, 40, 48–50, 51–52, 130, 135–38
self-expression, 77, 128, 222
importance of, 59
reticence of, 34, 63, 78
selfishness, 60, 127
self-mutilation, 32
self-theory, 20
separation, 73, 95
see also divorce
sex, sexual maturation, 195, 228–31
sexual harassment, 216
shame, 53, 55, 69, 75, 97, 98, 155, 176
discipline and, 104
shouting, 107, 108
Shure, Myrna, 22
shyness, 115
with adults, 33
low self-esteem and, 33
with peers, 33, 47, 180, 181
temperament and, 33
sibling rivalry, 21, 70, 79, 158–77
birth order and, 167–71
closeness of siblings and, 176–77
comparisons between siblings and, 161–64
desires of children and, 160
fairness and, 160, 165–66, 175–76
favoritism and, 160, 174, 177
gender bias and, 163–64
minimizing comparisons and, 164–67

nonconfrontational descriptions and, 164–65, 171
onset of, 160
parental expectations and, 163, 166–67
parental love and, 160
"perfect child" and, 166
physical violence and, 174, 176
praise and, 161–64
quarrels and, 171–75
siblings, 21, 28, 45, 49, 60, 79, 116
birth order of, 167–71
death of, 84
quarrels among, 171–75
step-, 172–73
twin, 170–71
social incompetence, 33, 47, 48
South Central (TV show), 161
Spivack, George, 22
sports, 90, 121, 135
standards, 126
high, 48–50, 51–52, 134
of performance, 130, 132–35, 157
self-esteem and, 157
setting of, 105, 109, 111
stress, 51, 95, 114
of parents, 72, 73, 77, 78, 80
structured conversations, 237–40
structured pep talk, 209–10
submissiveness, 35
success, 15
children's responses to, 14–15, 28
expectations of, 20, 38
humiliating experience and, 145
learning disabilities and, 152
low self-esteem and, 39–40
motivation and, 138
parents' emphasis on, 16–17
at school, *see* school
self-confidence and, 138, 140–41
triumph and, 15
suicide:
by adolescents, 221
humiliation and, 145
sulking, 77, 107